Lt. Elsie Ott's Top Secret Mission

This was the 1ST flight of a nurse, 6 patient from Karachi, India to Walter Reed hospital. Her patients involved polio case, Tuberculosis case, poss. the eye surgery, possible spinal surgery, a mute patient, etc. The flight lasted 6 1/2 days + they flew 13,000 miles. The problems encountered piracy a German

Lt. Elsie Ott's Top Secret Mission

plane hitting them with bullets, a wrestler needing a French surgery. Great character sketches. July 2021

The WWII Flight Nurse Pioneer of
Aeromedical Evacuation (MEDEVAC)

by

Jeffrey S. Copeland

PARAGON HOUSE

First Edition 2020

Published in the United States by
Paragon House
www.ParagonHouse.com

Cover Design by Mary Britt

Library of Congress Cataloging-in-Publication Data

Names: Copeland, Jeffrey S. (Jeffrey Scott), 1953- author.
Title: Lt. Elsie Ott's top secret mission : the WWII flight nurse pioneer
  of aeromedical evacuation (medevac) / by Jeffrey S. Copeland.
Other titles: WWII flight nurse pioneer of aeromedical evacuation (medevac)

Description: First edition. | [St. Paul] : Paragon House, 2020. | Summary:
  "Lt. Elsie Ott's historic, top-secret aeromedical evacuation mission in
  January of 1943 helped pave the way for a dramatic change in how wounded
  soldiers received vital medical care. Lt. Ott was given the task of
  transporting five severely wounded and ill soldiers from Karachi, India
  to Walter Reed Hospital in Washington, D.C. During this grueling
  journey, she and her patients faced German fighter planes, guerilla
  snipers, altitude challenges, logistical complications, and more."--
  Provided by publisher.
Identifiers: LCCN 2019044332 (print) | LCCN 2019044333 (ebook) | ISBN
  9781557789419 (paperback) | ISBN 9781610831222 (ebook)
Subjects: LCSH: Ott, Elsie S., 1913-2006. | Aviation nursing--United
  States--History--20th century. | Transport of sick and wounded--United
  States--History--20th century. | World War, 1939-1945--Participation,
  Female. | World War, 1939-1945--Medical care. | United States. Army
  Nurse Corps--History. | United States. Army Air Forces--History. |
  Nurses--Biography.
Classification: LCC D807.U6 C67 2020 (print) | LCC D807.U6 (ebook) | DDC
  940.54/7573--dc23
LC record available at https://lccn.loc.gov/2019044332
LC ebook record available at https://lccn.loc.gov/2019044333

Manufactured in the United States of America   10 9 8 7 6 5 4 3 2 1

The paper used in this publication meets the minimum requirements of
American National Standard for Information Sciences—Permanence of
Paper for Printed Library Materials, ANSIZ39.48-1984.

For my daughter, Crystal Lynn

Author's Note

TODAY, IT IS COMMON for airplanes and helicopters to transport individuals from hospital to hospital, to remove those who need care from accident scenes, to transport organs for transplant, and to deliver vital medical supplies when disasters strike. Who among us doesn't know of a friend, co-worker, relative, or loved one who has been touched in some way by these life-saving services?

According to the Association of Air Medical Services, over 550,000 medical aircraft transports occur each year—and the number is climbing steadily. Since WWII, aeromedical evacuation teams (today shortened to MEDEVAC) have been established all over the globe, providing medical care and coverage that has saved millions of lives.

And, the major spark for all of this began with the work of Lieutenant Elsie S. Ott. Lt. Ott sparked an evolution in medicine that has saved millions of lives in a period from just before the conclusion of WWII to the present. Though she was recognized for her pioneering work during her lifetime, today few beyond military historians recognize her name, and even fewer know the full story of her ground-breaking journey. Much of the work she did was tucked away for decades in classified military documents.

The adventure that follows is based on a true story, the details of which were gathered from archives, records centers, and military documents of the era. Because many of the records involved here are still classified, some names have been changed, and other characters are composites of several.

However, the bravery, heroism, and courage of the individuals presented here are real and described as they occurred during this historic mission.

JSC

Contents

Chapter 1

"No Use Worrying"

1825 ZULU, January 17, 1943
(51 miles east of Aden, Saudi Arabia)

LARGE PLUMES OF BLACK SMOKE erupted from the right engine, almost totally covering the center portion of the dull, silver wing.

Only moments before, our C-47 Transport had shuddered violently as we heard a low, gurgling sound followed by a series of loud pops that seemed to be coming from just outside the right bank of windows. The smoke followed almost instantly as what appeared to be a gas or oil ring expanded and arched all the way across the width of the wing, resembling a grass fire spreading rapidly in a swift wind.

I had started to scream when the C-47 suddenly picked up speed and banked downward as the right propeller stopped, and thick, now greyish-black smoke covered the windows. All happened so fast two of my patients lying on cots off to my left were thrown to the floor and rolled toward me, both of them crashing together at my ankles, causing me to topple back against the wall. Completely stunned, none of us uttered a sound.

Sergeant Rigazzi, who had been seated just ahead of me, held tight to a leather strap between the windows as he turned his head and stared my direction. His mouth opened as if he were going to speak, but before he could, the angle of our dive increased even more, slamming us together. His hand slipped from the strap. I grabbed his arm and pushed hard as I could, but he lost his balance and fell to the floor with a thud.

My ears plugged, so much so the roar of the engine became faint, like the steady, low drone of a truck motor at idle. I felt dizzy, a wave of nausea climbing my throat. Sergeant Rigazzi finally spoke, "Lieutenant Ott, what . . . What do we . . .?" I just shook my head and blew out three quick breaths. Our attention was drawn back to the floor as several dozen C-ration cans dislodged from their carton, rolled, and bounced toward us, settling around our feet.

Captain Goldman, my acute tuberculosis case, slumped in a chair anchored to the left wall next to where Sergeant Rigazzi had been only moments before. The angle of our descent caused his legs to dance back and forth on the floor in front of me. He appeared unconscious, but I couldn't tell if it was from injury or fright—or both.

Jerking my head to peer out the windows again, I saw the area covered by smoke had doubled in size and was moving toward the window directly in front of me. Our angle of descent was so severe I couldn't see the sky.

Out of the corner of my eye, I saw the co-pilot reach up and rip open the sheer curtains separating him and the pilot from the rest of us. I saw the pilot's right hand stiffen and roughly push forward the control next to his knee. While he did so, Private Scalini, who had tumbled awkwardly and head-first from his seat, clutched my legs and moaned as a thick, perfectly circular pool of blood formed around his head. He looked up at me, his eyes pleading. I couldn't move, but not because of the steepness of our dive. I was frozen by the unknown of the moment and dug the heels of my shoes into the floor while arching even tighter against the side of the plane.

In the midst of this chaos, my mind shot back to the words of Nurse Rose McCall, Head Nurse at Barksdale Army Air Field Station Hospital in Louisiana, where I had been given my final training before being shipped overseas. The day Nurse McCall found out I was to be stationed in India, she took me aside and offered several pieces of advice, part of which had to do with the perils of travel, especially flight. "I've traveled all over the world in my day," she said. "And I can tell you nothing will age you like being aboard a plane. But you can't worry about it. Doesn't do any good. Won't matter."

"What in the world do you mean?" I had asked, perplexed by how serious her words had been.

She smiled slightly. "What I mean is a lot of these floating coffins we have in the air come crashing down. But, as I said, you can't worry about that. If your plane does hit the ground, the odds are almost certain you'll be dead. That's what I mean. So, when it's your turn to fly, just climb on in and relax. No use worrying."

Her voice echoed through my still plugged ears as I turned again and stared out the window just below my right shoulder. Even though we were still at fair altitude and I had to squint through the thick smoke, I could see the outline of a small mountain. With the shrill roar of the left engine increasing second by second and the ground drawing closer and closer, my mind raced. "This is it," I thought. "We're going down."

∾

Chapter 2

"All Her Fault"

A Month Earlier
0701 ZULU, December 17, 1942
Allied Supreme Regional Headquarters
China-Burma-India Theater
Bombay, India

"General, why are there so many MPs with machine guns outside the door? Why did I have to show my tags and ID twice just to get in here? I was practically given the third degree." Captain Edward Walters of the 181st Evacuation Hospital took a chance when he interrupted the meeting just called to order by General Albert Baxter, Deputy Director of the Office of the Air Surgeon.

Obviously, others shared this curiosity as a low rumble spread across the room. It stopped suddenly as Captain Walters sat back down under the general's withering scowl. General Baxter was a gruff tank of a man who looked more like a prize-fighter than the skilled surgeon he was. His face was weathered, lined, hard. Standing at six feet, six inches tall and weighing in close to two hundred and forty pounds, he knew his size intimidated others and used that to his advantage.

Having regained the full attention of the twenty-three officers of the U.S. Army Air Forces sitting before him, he began.

"Since security seems to be a concern, let's address that. When the doors closed, we went into top secret session, and they won't open again until our business is done. You were invited here because you're darn good at what you do, and we need your expertise. You didn't realize it before, but all of you volunteered for this meeting, which, by the way, isn't taking place. You're here by order of the big man himself, General Grant, to offer consultation on a plan of ours we'd like to get started on right away."

The men exchanged looks, and most sat up smartly in their chairs. General David Grant, the Air Surgeon, was one of the most powerful and influential officers of the Allied forces. Everyone in the room was under his direct command, so they knew they had better pay attention.

Most opened notebooks and poised themselves to jot notes as General Baxter continued. "General Grant and a few others of us have a plan, a vision, and you're going to help us make it work. As you well know, General Grant and our Surgeon General, General Magee, don't see eye to eye on most things. What we're going to talk about now is one of those areas, and if word of this meeting leaked out to the Surgeon General's Office, General Grant would be cooked, and it wouldn't do the rest of us—all of you included—any good, either. Gentlemen, that's why the secrecy. That's why the security today."

He withdrew a stack of papers from under the podium where he stood and held them up. "Let's get down to brass tacks. Let me give you the latest statistics from the reports put together last week. We know for a fact when one of our boys gets medical treatment within the first five hours after being hurt, his chances of survival increase by six-hundred percent. Six-hundred percent! Let that soak in a minute."

"This percentage is for what we call *regular* wounds and injuries. Our job is to get 'em treated and back to the lines or on their way home. We work fast, and we're definitely good at that. The mortality rate for those who get care within that five-hour window is declining all the time. But what about the wounded who can't be seen within that small window? And what about those who need specialized care we can't do ourselves, that we don't have the expertise and facilities for?"

The general tolerated the silence that met his questions for a few seconds before slamming the report down on the table, startling those next to him. "Too many of our boys die unnecessarily because we can't do our jobs the way we're supposed to. The number of soldiers we're losing before they receive proper medical attention is staggering and *unacceptable*. These latest reports disgust me as they should you, too."

Captain Oscar Wilmington, Chief Surgeon of the 187th General Hospital, took a chance and stood up. "Believe me, Sir, we think about this all the time, but here in the CBI Theater, we can't in good conscience promise our troops if they're injured we'll be able to get them the help they'll need to survive within those five hours. In the first place, the roads around here and all across to Burma look mostly like goat paths, not fit for our transport trucks to haul the wounded. Windblown sand closes them up nearly every night most places, and the jungles are so dense throughout the rest of the Theater it takes squads of men with machetes and axes to keep the roads even half-way open. And the trains everywhere in the region are jokes and aren't used much at all. Ships? We don't control the waters around here enough to make them an option. This whole part of the world is one big transportation snafu, and nobody has figured out what to do about it."

His face tightening, General Baxter slammed his fist on the podium and motioned Captain Wilmington to sit down. His voice rising, he replied, "I know the problems here, and they're the same everywhere else we're fighting. Most of what you say is true. But, there's one area where we couldn't be more different in our thinking. It doesn't have to be 'just the way it is.' If this is the best we can do, if we give up and continue to have these unnecessary sacrifices, we're not fit to call ourselves doctors."

After this last remark, a roar swelled across the room, and several shouted, "Wait a minute!" and "That's not fair!"

Colonel Andrew Smithers, Commander of the 112th Station Hospital in Karachi, stood, used the backs of his legs to push back his chair, and said loudly enough to be heard above the commotion, "Hold on! All of us can admit there have been many times we look at a patient and see him slip away while thinking to ourselves, 'If only he could be sent to a specialist, he might have a chance to survive.' However, we're not to blame in these situations. We're not equipped to handle these cases, and we can't get them the proper care fast enough. If only we could . . ."

General Baxter cut him off, but did so with a slight smile. "Sit down, Andrew. I appreciate your sentiments. I'll take it from here. Gentlemen, Colonel Smithers couldn't have said it better. He said, 'We can't get them the proper care fast enough.' *That's* why we're here."

Looking around the room and seeing the irritation on too many faces, he continued, "Well, if nothing else, I've got your full attention, and that's what I want. Keep an open mind now for a few minutes. General Grant has stuck his neck out with a plan to help our wounded, to dramatically speed up how quickly we can get them care."

Walking out from behind the podium and looking once around the room, the general shot his right arm straight up and announced, "We're taking to the sky! How does a fleet of air ambulances sound to you? How about if the wounded could be transported in a matter of hours over distances that would take days, in some cases weeks, by truck or train? How about if those who need specialized care could actually receive it in time to do some good? How about if you had hundreds of specially trained nurses, who could give you extra support with this? General Grant wants to call this the first 'Air Evacuation Service,' supported by Medical Air Ambulance Squadrons. How does that sound to all of you?"

No one moved. Then Captain Simon Goldbaum of the 49th Port Surgical Hospital stood and started applauding, quietly at first, then as fast and loudly as he could. Almost instantly, everyone in the room followed suit. Captain Walters of the 181st was the first to speak. "It's about time somebody picked up this torch again. I've been asking for this the whole time I've been over here."

General Baxter, obviously pleased by the men's support, said, "Yes, Captain, we believe we can do this effectively and efficiently, so much so that all of you are going to help us pull this off once we put on a little demonstration."

Seeing the interest and excitement in their eyes, he pushed ahead. "We've been in an uphill battle so far. The Surgeon General has been outspoken in his opposition to air ambulances. On the other side, General Grant knows this can work and is willing to risk his career to prove it. We can't let him down, or this idea will die again.

"So, here's what we're going to do. General Grant and I

decided we need a dramatic example, an *experiment* of such magnitude every single one of the higher-ups—all the way to the President—will stand up and take notice. I've brought with me this morning a few men to fill you in on everything we can think of for this experiment. If this works, all of you will be on the Task Force to continue the effort."

"The first to speak to you this morning has been around for a while. I don't *think* there's any truth to the rumor he was there to hand wrenches to the Wright Brothers when they got that thing off the ground at Kitty Hawk, but I can't be sure. I know for a fact he was one of our first daredevil pilots. Fortunately for us, he gave that up and went into medicine, probably so he could sew himself up after all the crashes he had. So, here is Captain Tad Townsend, Chief Surgeon of 98th Station Hospital in Chakulin—still with us."

As he walked to the podium, Captain Townsend said, drolly, "Wright Brothers? Very funny, General." He directed his attention to those before him. "Good morning, Gentlemen. I actually flew an old Jenny in the war back in Eighteen when some of you here weren't even born. It's because I'm still above ground that General Baxter asked me to say a few words of history to you."

A few spread note pads before them. Others adjusted themselves more comfortably in their chairs. When he had everyone's full attention, Captain Townsend began. "Did you know the first reported use of moving wounded soldiers by air actually took place in balloons during the Franco- Prussian War and later in our own American Civil War? It didn't amount to much and wasn't practical, but it put thoughts in heads, thoughts that kept churning as years went by.

"Back in Seventeen, the British tried making air ambulances, but all they really ended up with was a contraption to strap the wounded to the wings of their ships. Gave those poor boys one heck of a ride. If their wounds didn't kill 'em, the fright from being on that wing sure could have. Can you imagine that?"

Most couldn't, and their laughter showed it.

"The Brits were also the first to attack rough terrain that prevented movement of the wounded. At the Sinai Peninsula, they gave some an hour plane ride across nothing but sand dunes that would have taken almost four days by camel. I did some of this myself in my Jenny when I was flying in Eighteen. One time I crammed two with serious leg wounds back behind me. They were in there like sardines, but both lived and both legs were saved. So, I've seen this can work first-hand."

"Most of you have heard about the off and on trials we've had moving casualties in the North Africa Campaign. The Germans are trying this, too, but from what I've heard, they're treating the wounded like cargo rather than patients because they're not taking care of them along the flight. I can't say much for our own current efforts, either. But, gentlemen, this is about to change. We now have equipment that will work for exactly this purpose. Make no mistake about it, this all has to start with the planes we use now. And, we have the perfect ship that will be the answer to our prayers. This may come as a surprise to some of you, but the C-47 is what we need and what we're going to use."

Again, a low rumble spread around the room. "I know what some of you are thinking. Our brothers-in-arms over in the Pacific have nicknamed this ship the Gooney Bird because, well, it looks like one. Like an Albatross flappin' its long wings while trying to take off. Make no mistake about it, the C-47 may look like it'd never get off the ground, but it's tough as nails and just as versatile. I've taken off in one of these on a rocky strip of ground no longer than a football field and landed one time in weather that was so foul we bounced like a ball all the way down the runway. But the ship always holds together. It's almost impossible to kill these things.

"But, that isn't why we like them for this. They're a complete refitting of the civilian Douglas DC-3, so they have plenty of room inside. Once we took out the regular seats and put in fold-down benches, we realized we could transport twenty-eight to thirty combat troops and fourteen to sixteen stretcher patients—and at least half a dozen more if they're ambulatory at all. We've used them before for this on a limited basis, with some success, but we don't have any official reports from medical folks about how feasible it is to build on that. That's part of what we want to do now—get some facts, some details.

"I'm not trying to sell this as a luxury liner, but I will say this. The C-47 will get patients where they're being sent quickly, efficiently, and safely—and much better than any of our other options right now. Of course, I'll admit this ship can't do everything. We're not going to use it for crossing the Atlantic, for example, although it probably could. We're working on larger planes for that—a story for another time. Well, Gentlemen, that is all I have to say. Any questions?"

"Just one," Captain Wilmington said, raising his hand. "I think you've sold us on the plane and what it can do, but where do we fit into all this? Are you building this up because we are going to be right there with the wounded on these planes? If so, I at least want a guarantee of a darn parachute."

Plenty of laughs followed his words, but it was also clear others had the same thought. The doctors now leaned forward as if afraid they might miss the response to the question.

"You're a little ahead of yourself, Sir," Captain Townsend said, making a quick glance at General Baxter. "I suppose it's possible some of you might get air under your feet a time or two, but don't get too anxious just yet. Wait until you hear the rest. And, trust me–if you want a parachute, I'll personally get you one."

Colonel Baxter sensed the unease that had filled the room and stood. "Thank you, Tad. Good information. Let's move on and talk about some specifics of the *experiment*. I want you to hear exactly what's going to happen next month."

Picking up a pointer, the general moved to the large map on the wall behind him. He raised the pointer. "Follow this, closely." Slowly he traced a zig-zag route from India across the globe to a point about half-way down the Eastern Seaboard of the United States.

"Now what I'm about to say absolutely can't leave this room. The only reason I'm sharing part of the route with you now is we'd like your input about possible alternative stops. We've looked at this dozens of times, and every time we come up with the same hospitals. If you can think of better places along the way, we want to hear about them."

He again saw curious faces before him, so he walked out in front of the podium, slapped the pointer to his leg and said, loudly, "We plan to take about half a dozen special-case patients by plane that whole distance I just drew—from Karachi to Walter Reed in Washington. That's going to be our experiment, and if we pull it off, that's how we'll get the attention—and support—of all."

The exclamations, while muted as if some were partially in disbelief, filled the room. These were followed by questions that came in chorus. "Can it really be done?" "Who's taking them?" "Who, exactly, is going?" One doctor at the back began applauding while others turned to stare his direction. Even Captain Wilmington, the biggest skeptic in the room, slowly clapped his hands together and nodded his approval. Soon, applause erupted from all.

"Hold on," General Baxter interrupted. "Before you get too excited, understand this isn't going to be a cake-walk by any means. We've contacted several hospitals on this route already, and they've agreed to provide aid as needed. They don't know why we want this special help, just that we'll be grateful for their cooperation. They've pledged it, and we're counting on it. But if they don't come through, well, we could be in trouble."

General Baxter returned to the map and indicated each proposed stop by snapping the pointer loudly at the spot on the map. "Here's what we have so far. First stop, Aden, Arabia. Next, on to El Fasher. If all continues to go as planned, the next stop will be our 67th Station Hospital at Accra in the Gold Coast Colony. That's where they'll change planes. After that, they'll cross the Atlantic and head to Natal, Brazil. From there, after a few refueling stops, they'll be on U.S. soil. Then they'll shoot up to Walter Reed."

Smiling broadly, he turned to face the group again. "And just how long do you think this journey will take? What are your guesses?"

The responses came quickly, one after the other. "Three weeks!" "No, depending the needs of the patients, I'd say close to a month." "Five weeks!" shouted another. Still others were making charts on their notepads and counting silently to themselves.

General Baxter drew them back together again by announcing, loudly, "One week. That's all. If we're going to prove anything, it had better be dramatic or most of the Brass will say something like, 'Nice job. We'll take it under advisement.' We can't have that. We've got to get enough ammunition back to General Grant and the Air Surgeon's office that they can hold this up and say, 'Look, we proved this can be done in extreme travel circumstances over great distance, so think of what it could mean in general practice. Think of the lives we can save.'

"And to answer the earlier question, doctors aren't going to be riding along in our plan. If—no when this works—we're going to start a special training program to create a new type of aviation flight nurse, one who can perform all the duties and care required until the patients get where they need to be. So, all of you can relax. You won't be tagging along."

At the mention of the nurses, a few raised hands, but he motioned for them to be lowered. "There will be time for questions, but let's finish up the details of the mission. For this, I'm now going to turn it over to Colonel Samuel Leiter, Commander of the 159th Station Hospital in Karachi. We've consulted with him at length, and he's come up with the nurse who is going to be in charge of and who will take care of the patients all the way back home. Colonel Leiter, would you please step forward. The floor is yours."

Colonel Leiter opened a folder, placed it on the podium. "My job this morning is to introduce you to the individual who will be assigned to carry out this mission. Second Lieutenant Elsie S. Ott. Serial Number N727991. Twenty-nine years old.

One hundred and twenty pounds. Five feet and three inches. Graduated 1936 from Lenox Hill Hospital School of Nursing in New York City. A fine school. Surgical assistance training in 1938 at St. Francis Hospital, Miami, Florida. Top of her class there. Commissioned Army Air Force Nurse Corps in September 1941. Assigned initially Barksdale Army Air Field Station Hospital, New Orleans, Louisiana. Head Ward Nurse there and trained all new nurses. Was good at it, too. Requested overseas duty and was assigned to the 159th Station Hospital. On top of this . . ."

At this point, Captain Ranse Howard, Chief Medical Officer for the local 506th General Hospital, interrupted him by clearing his throat loudly enough to gain the attention of all. He folded his arms and asked, irritation clearly filling his words, "Come on, Samuel. Get to the point. She seems competent. Good training. Good record. But, at the same time, she really doesn't sound all that different from a dozen other nurses you and I could list right now. So, why her? What makes her so special?"

Colonel Leiter smiled and replied, "First and foremost, we need someone who has a real chance to pull this off. Someone tough and who can take it if things start to muck up. We've checked her out six ways from Sunday, and she's definitely all that.

"But it's exactly *because* she also sounds like the dozen others you know that makes her *perfect*. Sir, you have just said what we're hoping others will say. Right now, there *are* dozens of others who could do this, and that's exactly the point we hope to prove. We want people saying 'If *she* can do this, there's no reason we can't find plenty of other nurses to do the same thing.'

We believe we can train nurses to perform this service and don't think it would take long to get groups of them ready—*if* this mission pans out and Lt. Ott comes through for us."

General Baxter stood and Colonel Leiter returned to his seat. "Thanks, Samuel. I'll take it from here—and fill in the *impatient*." There were a few more nervous laughs as all eyes focused on Captain Howard. "Here's the rest of the answer to your question. She doesn't stick out from a crowd. By all accounts, she does her work, does it well, and never makes waves or causes the least bit of trouble. She also doesn't have any family to speak of other than her mother. In short, I doubt anyone would miss her if she were gone."

There were more than a few light gasps and whispered questions that sprang up across the room. Quickly, he continued. "Oh, I don't exactly mean nobody would miss her if she died while doing this, although that might be true. What I mean is there's always a chance this experiment of ours won't work. A lot of bad things could happen. Patients could die en route. The plane could go down. Lt. Ott could snap under the pressure."

Captain George Branacke, Chief Surgeon of the 503rd Station Hospital, raised a hand. "Sir, seems to me like you're putting all your eggs in one basket for something this important. What if something really does happen along the way? This is a lot of pressure to put on her shoulders."

General Baxter and Colonel Leiter glanced at each other, each slightly smiling, before General Baxter said, "Don't disagree with you at all, George. That's why we're going to hedge our bets a little. We're sending along a medic—just in case. He'll be there if needed, but we hope he'll just be along for the ride. Plus, we're going to give Ott a document to keep with her at all times. We'll call it a 'Wild Card' letter. If she gets into any type of serious trouble, that letter will be signed by so many important pieces of Brass any and all doors should open for her. She'll be instructed not to use it unless absolutely necessary because of the secrecy here, but it'll be there in case."

Looking around the room again to make sure he had the attention of all, he added, this time his voice more stern, "Listen *if* this *does* go bad, it will probably be the fault of the nurse. The nurse. If this all goes south, it might be all her fault. Not ours."

After General Baxter's last comment, many in the room shook their heads and shifted in their chairs.

"On the other hand, if this is a success—and I believe this all can work—it will all have been our idea, and we'll look pretty darn smart. Get my meaning now?"

General Baxter pointed off to his right. "Captain Rogers, also from the 159th, is now going to talk to you about another one of the important parts of this mission. Captain Rogers, please take over."

Captain Rogers walked to the podium and began. "I'm going to tell you about those who will be taken back to Washington on this trial run. There are a couple of important considerations here. First, we'll take patients who need long-term care, those we can't and shouldn't deal with over here. We want them to be ill, but not *too* ill. Plus, it would be good to show a range of afflictions to demonstrate we can handle all sorts of issues. I'd like some litter-bound and some ambulatory. The bottom line is we are going to stack the deck and try to go with those who have the greatest chance of getting there alive. Would look pretty bad if we lost some. So, a couple of days before the sendoff, I'll look through the charts at the 159th and select those I feel qualify. General, That's it from me. Anything you want to add?"

General Baxter looked around the room once again. "Before we adjourn, I've just a couple more things. First, we look to have the mission begin about mid-January. The actual date will depend on the reports we get from North Africa. There's still a shootin' war going on there. No use putting them in harm's way unnecessarily. Second, I want each of you to prepare a report for me with your recommendations and general thoughts on how we can best make this work, especially about appropriate stops along the way. Think hard—do you know anyone at any of the hospitals along this route? Anyone you can recommend for us in case extra help is needed during the mission? I want this information fast. Like tomorrow afternoon at the latest. And, keep it strictly on a 'need to know' basis. We want to get rolling, so all of you get busy. Any questions?"

Giving them virtually no time to respond, he waved the pointer one last time. "Good! Now, let's get out of here. We've all much to do."

As everyone stood to leave, Captain Wilmington leaned over to Captain Smithers and said, "I'd sure hate to be that nurse."

Captain Smithers smiled and replied, "Yeah, but better her than us."

∾

Chapter 3

Sabotage!

1831 ZULU, January 17
(37 miles east of Aden, Saudi Arabia)

Other than a shrill "crack, crack, crack" heard coming through the smoke still billowing from the right engine, all was eerily silent inside the cabin until the pilot started barking orders. We were all still—so frozen in fear we could only hold fast to whatever we could grab and listen as he shouted observations and commands to the co-pilot and radio operator.

The plane leveled off slightly as he said, loudly enough for all of us to hear, "Broken gas line. Pretty sure. No fire yet—that's some good luck. Pull mixture to idle. Cut fuel supply. Shut off fuel selector."

I could see the pilot's forearms straining, bulging as he fought to keep the controls steady.

He turned again to the co-pilot and said, urgently, "Engage engine fire extinguisher! Let's coat it down—just in case. That should help."

Through the window just above my shoulder I could see the smoke dying away as a milky-white liquid sprayed out from the engine housing and coated the wing. I started to point this out to Sergeant Rigazzi, but before I could, the pilot shouted again, his voice growing deeper and more clipped.

"All right, boys, nose down. Let's pick up what speed we can to keep it starved. Here we go!"

Instantly we were in another steep dive, this one even more sharp than the first. Rigazzi appeared to be looking right through me as he shouted, "What the . . . Enough of this! Level off!"

The swift descent lasted for maybe half a minute at best but felt much longer. Finally, the pilot called out, "OK, gear down, wheels down. Slow us up—and hang on."

The dive ended abruptly as the nose of the ship rose up, causing something like a floating sensation. At that instant, my stomach felt like it had climbed up through my throat. The nausea spread equally as fast, and I fought it as best I could. Our speed seemed to drop by at least half, which scared us so badly I heard a collective gasp from the others. Looking out the window again, I saw the smoke was completely gone.

We settled into a rhythmic bouncing, up and down, side to side. The sensation reminded me of riding in a fast-moving car over a deeply rutted gravel road. It was not so distracting that I didn't notice the pilot had lowered his voice so I could no longer hear him. This frightened me more than ever.

I looked down, and Private Scalini was still clutching at my leg as the blood ring around his head continued to expand. I had completely forgotten about him. To stabilize us more, I tried moving forward to grab hold of one of the litter brackets on the side wall of the plane, but my skirt was stuck fast to a seat support behind me. I was trapped—couldn't move forward or back. I kicked my left leg to try to free myself, but when I did my foot accidentally caught Private Scalini smack in the ribs. His eyes opened wide, his head tilted back, and the expression on his face screamed, "Why?"

Shaking my head to indicate I was sorry, I reached down and yanked hard as I could at the back of my dress. I heard a drawn-out rip and was free. However, when the plane suddenly and violently rocked left again, down I went, hard, my right shoulder smashing to the floor. As the plane immediately swung back to the right, so did we, all crashing heavily against the wall.

Finally able to find a hand hold, I climbed back up so I could check my other patients. Either they hadn't been tossed around as much as I had been, or they had been flung back to their original positions. None spoke as my eyes met theirs. There was nothing at that point for any of us to say.

The co-pilot broke the silence. Craning his neck around the cockpit opening, he shouted back toward us, "All of you! Listen up now! Full attention!"

The high-pitched roar of the left engine made it difficult to hear him, so I swung myself around so I could see his lips as he spoke.

"We look OK now, but we're going to need your help with a couple things. First, any of you who can, grab one of the fire extinguishers strapped between the windows."

The pilot said something to him I couldn't make out, and he quickly turned again to face us. "Take all sharp objects out of your pockets and stow 'em if you can. I make us just under five miles from the field, so grab something. Hold tight and don't let go. I know you're scared, but we've done this before and we're still here. We'll get us down. No need to panic. Just hang on. I'll let you know in a minute if there's anything else to do."

I was taken completely by surprise when his face softened, and he actually smiled. Looking directly at me, he said, "Oh, and one more thing. If you start getting too scared, just take off your shoes and count your toes. By the time you get to ten, or whatever you have, we'll be taxiing down the runway. Now, get ready."

It was so silly, the laughter just poured right out of me. Same with Sergeant Rigazzi, who had finally righted himself and was checking to make sure our patients were ready. "Lieutenant," he said to me, "I'll keep watch over here. You fine over there?"

I nodded. "And say a prayer or two while you're at it. Couldn't hurt, right?" Leaning down, I said to Private Scalini, whose hands were still clutched to my ankle, "Please, grab that handle there instead. I need to be able to move."

Without saying a word, he let loose of his grip, grabbed his still-bleeding head with his left hand and used the right to crawl over to where he could steady himself. "You'll be fine," I said, in a tone I immediately regretted, one that practically shouted, "Not sure I truly believe that myself." He smiled weakly up at me and closed his eyes.

Just over a minute or so later, the pilot abruptly increased the engine speed, which caused the nose to rise for a moment, startling us again. The co-pilot turned toward us one last time and shouted, "Hang on—tight! We're taking her down!"

Through the window I could see a small clump of trees just a few feet below us. I started to point them out to Sergeant Rigazzi, but before I could, I felt a jolt that snapped us sharply forward. I fought to keep myself righted and again dug my heels into the floor. We bounced side to side down the landing strip until the pilot eased us to the right and slowed smoothly until we came to a stop. After shutting down the left engine, the pilot stood, swung around, and with the radio operator close behind exited through the forward door.

I was still so stunned I couldn't move. Sergeant Rigazzi raised his hands and shouted, to no one in particular, "Another of the nine lives used up! Dodged a bullet again. Thank, God!"

"You can say that again," the co-pilot responded while laughing and moving toward us. "Anybody hurt back here? How about you, Lieutenant? You count your toes?"

I didn't have time to reply. I ran to the back of the plane, knelt toward the corner, and started throwing up.

"Can't say as I blame her," I heard Sergeant Rigazzi say. "Surprised we're all not down there with her. What a landing! Actually, I have a question for you. Did we land—or did we crash? Hard for me to tell."

The co-pilot laughed heartily. "A little of both, I think. At least that's what my stomach says. But, I wasn't too worried. These Gooney Birds can land on a postage stamp with one wing knotted up. I just hope the damage isn't bad."

I didn't turn around but could tell he was addressing me, "First time losing your chow on a landing? Don't feel bad."

I wiped my mouth. "Yes, it is. And my first time on a plane, too—ever. Does this kind of landing happen often?"

"First time?" he said, laughing again. "Maiden voyage. Well, I'll be darned. Well, yes, about one out of two landings will go something like this. You'll get used to it."

Finally ready to stand again, I turned and saw him wink at Sergeant Rigazzi. "I'm not worried about your landings," I said. "What I want to know is this." Now, my voice almost pleading, I asked, "Can we keep on schedule? Got to be off again tomorrow."

"We'll get us rolling again. Don't you worry about it. These birds are also easy to work on. Wasn't any fire, so shouldn't be too bad. You take care of your patients. That's your job. We'll do ours."

With that, he turned the latch and swung open the large cargo door to our left. Lowering a metal ladder, he started climbing down. I turned to Sergeant Rigazzi and, now half-way composed again, said, "Let's check 'em out. We'll do it here before we worry about transport to the base hospital. Start with the two closest to you, and I'll take the rest. Sing out if you need help."

"I'm on it, Lieutenant. You can count on me."

My patients were in pretty good shape considering what we'd just been through. The large ring of blood around Private Scalini's head turned out to be from a shallow scalp wound. I shouldn't have been shocked by the size of the pool; nothing bleeds quite like a head wound. I cleaned the area, applied a small bandage, and he was good to go. The others, especially my litter patients, were shook up but hadn't incurred any additional injury. Once I had determined they needed no more immediate care, I motioned for Sergeant Rigazzi to follow me down the ladder so we could visit off to ourselves.

As soon as our feet hit the ground, a member of the ground crew walked over and asked if there was anything he could do to help out. I told him we needed to figure out a way to get the patients to the base hospital, and he said he could arrange a truck if we wouldn't mind waiting ten minutes or so. That sounded fine, so I instructed Sergeant Rigazzi to pull up a couple of crates so we could sit and be comfortable while waiting.

Our first priority was to go over the patient charts. Neither of us had given more than a passing glance at them because we had been so pressed for time before takeoff at Karachi.

"So, what do we have?" he asked, handing me the charts. "Why these men? Why do they get the ride?"

"We're about to find out," I replied. "I guess we'll only know what's in here."

I skimmed through all the charts as quickly as I could and read the important sections aloud to Sergeant Rigazzi. We had five patients, all with very different medical circumstances. Our first litter patient was Lieutenant Jerome Collins, age thirty-four, who was afflicted with recent-onset chronic poliomyelitis. The chart indicated paralysis had set in at his lower extremities and left arm. A special note attached said he was also an Army Air Forces pilot who had flown a P-38 Lightning in Burma and had six kills to his credit. He was being taken back home not just for treatment, but also to receive several medals for valor.

The second litter patient was Private Andrew Montague. He was experiencing paralysis below the waist as the result of multiple lumbar vertebrae fractures. Complicating that, he had four broken ribs, a fractured left shoulder blade, and a broken right wrist. The notes explained he had been driving a troop evacuation truck out of Burma when it crossed over a mine in the road. He was behind the wheel at the time and was the only survivor of the explosion. The bouncing we had just received must have caused him excruciating pain, but he never let out so much as a yelp.

Patient three was Captain Sidney Goldman, who had been Chief Dental Surgeon at the 112th Station Hospital in Karachi. He was experiencing a very nasty case of early, active tuberculosis. The chart indicated recent symptoms were bloody cough, regular chest pain when breathing, extreme fatigue, high fever, and sweats followed by chills. The notes indicated he was being taken back for treatment at a special sanatorium in Virginia.

Next on the list was Private Anthony Scalini. The cracked scalp he had just received was the least of his problems. He was listed as having "glaucoma, both eyes, with 60 interocular pressure." Any significant increase in eye pressure above that and his eyes could simply explode like stepped-on grapes. His vision was currently quite blurry and, hopefully, it would stay exactly that way along the journey. He was being taken back for specialized treatment at Walter Reed Hospital. There were no extra notes in his folder other than the fact he preferred to be called Tony.

Our last patient was Corporal Edward Ernst, whose chart indicated, "battle fatigue, manic depressive, nonviolent." He was also being sent for treatment at Walter Reed. According to the notes in his chart, he had been a supply convoy driver in Burma until he was captured. The Japanese had starved and tortured him. He finally escaped and made his way through the jungle on a journey that took just over a month. When back in Allied territory, he reported vital information about Japanese camps and air strips. The day after making his report, he collapsed and hasn't spoken since. He apparently is still alert to all around him, but his communication is nothing more than nods, weak smiles, and an occasional bout of tears.

When I finished the charts, Sergeant Rigazzi shook his head and said, "I see they didn't give you the sixth chart. Wonder how come?"

He slowly removed his helmet, and as he did so I got my first close look at his face. He was quite a good-looking man. His auburn hair was curly – and was accentuated by his dark-brown eyes and thick eyebrows. He had a beautiful and warm smile. He was also very tall and muscular.

When I finally stopped admiring his looks, I asked, "What sixth chart? What are you talking about? There are only five patients, right?"

"Not exactly," he said, lowering his head. "Technically, *I'm* the sixth. It's true I've been trained as a medic, and they wanted me here because they think I can help you take care of these men. At the same time, they couldn't figure out what to do with me, so they're also sending me back to see if a change in climate does me any good. You see, I've got chronic arthritis that gets so bad at times I can't move these arms. I don't always feel it. As a matter of fact, I'm fine now—and hope to be the rest of the way back. Personally, I think it's this stinkin' climate that's eating me up. My bet is some good, American sunshine will do the trick. You should also know they're not booting me out. I'm just being reassigned back to the States."

"Good for you!" I replied. "A change of scene will be good for us all." Looking up at the plane, I added, "Let's just get there in one piece."

After an awkward moment of silence, I asked, "Sergeant, I don't even know your full name. What do you go by?"

"My name's Samuel, but everyone back home just calls me Sam. Please call me that, Lieutenant. I'd appreciate it."

"I'm Elsie." I extended my hand to shake his. "Feel free to use that when we're not in formal settings. I hope we'll be pals. Lord knows we'll need each other if we're going to get through this."

He offered me a cigarette, but I waved it away. As he put the pack away, I asked, "By the way, Sam, how much in advance did you know about this mission? I didn't know until less than twenty-four hours before when I was simply informed I'd be involved. How about you?"

"Same here," he said. "Caught me completely by surprise. Oh, I knew I'd likely be sent home sooner than later, but I had no idea I'd be assigned to a top secret mission like this. I still don't understand completely what this is all about. The Captain said only that I was supposed to give you all the help I could and see that you got home safely. That was it. I still feel pretty much in the dark."

"Me, too. I guess they don't want us to know too much, and right now that's fine with me. This is the Army, after all. When they want us to know, they'll tell us. That's always the way it is."

Just then, a jeep pulled up right in front of us. A young British private looked over at me and asked, "You Lieutenant Ott?" When I nodded, he continued, "I'm Private Clive. You're supposed to come with me. Hospital Chief wants to see you. Said you're to come now, and transport will be here shortly for your patients. Please hop in."

"Go ahead," Sam said, motioning me toward the jeep. "I'll stay with 'em while you get things sorted out. Not to worry."

"I'll hurry them up," I said, climbing in the jeep. "Thanks, Sergeant. Appreciate it."

≈

When the British General Hospital first came into view, I blew out a breath and said, "Impressive. Very impressive."

Private Clive downshifted, laughed, and said, "Lieutenant, I think that's putting it mildly."

cotton and a thick roll of gauze. "Here," he said, handing me the cotton. "Be careful and light with your touch, but place those as close as you can to the wood and hold them there."

After I had done so, he wrapped the gauze tightly round and round until the cotton was held firmly in place. When he finished, he said, "Normally, I'd get some salts and bring her around, but I don't want her moving just yet. Do your best, won't you, to keep her in that position."

Dr. Symington stood again, walked as close as he could get to the debris blocking the entrance, and called out, "Wounded in here! Get a suite ready in another wing when possible. Not an emergency case, but still necessary to do when we can. Please acknowledge."

A different voice this time called back, "Acknowledged. Will pass it along."

He came back, knelt next to Nurse Martin, and carefully picked up her wrist to check her pulse. As he did so, she slowly opened her eyes and said, "What . . . What . . ."

"Just sit easy," Dr. Symington said calmly, as he continued noting her pulse. "Only a bit of flotsam. Nothing to fret about. We'll attend to it shortly. Just relax now."

I took her other hand and squeezed it gently. "That's right. Nothing serious. You'll be dancin' a jig again in no time."

Both of them gave me an odd look. Dr. Symington shook his head and said, "You Yanks always have the humor. I'll grant you that."

"We have to," I shot back. "To balance out you stodgy Brits." It was out of my mouth before I knew it, and I hoped I hadn't offended them too badly.

Nurse Martin laughed first, and Dr. Symington followed

a few seconds later. *"Stodgy,"* he said, looking me up and down. "Stodgy?"

The laughter was good for us—and especially for Nurse Martin, who appeared to have forgotten about her leg a few moments.

"When the going falls to rough," Dr. Symington said, still laughing, "British people like to engage in a light bit of story swapping. We might as well give it a go as it looks we'll be here a few ticks longer. With your permissions, I'll go first."

Destroying completely my first impression of him, Dr. Symington suddenly became warm and engaging as he regaled us with story after story of his days in medical college. I wouldn't say they were exactly rib-ticklers, but all were very light-hearted and entertaining. After telling us of a time when a fellow class-mate dumped a box of alum in a bowl of punch at a dance, causing everyone there to pucker for the rest of the evening, Dr. Symington fell into a fit of laughter so prolonged that Nurse Martin and I found the good doctor more humorous than the story itself.

Nurse Martin jumped in and said, "I've one for you. On the way home from Brighton one afternoon when I was but seventeen, I stepped without looking onto the motorway and was struck by a chimney sweep's lorry."

She laughed so hard both the doctor and I glanced down to make sure the bandaging was still secure. When she didn't continue her story, I looked at her and asked, "That's it? That's your funny tale? Being hit by a truck?"

When she could compose herself enough to reply, she said, "No, silly. I was fine. Barely a scratch. The lorry swerved after, hit the curb, and rolled over. Everyone on the sidewalk—must have been a good dozen of 'em—got a face full of ashes and coal dust. Black as pitch—all of 'em. But that's not the best part. That's how I met my boyfriend. He got the blackest face of all, and I helped wipe him off, and it was romance from that moment on."

Doctor Symington and I looked at each other and burst out laughing. Nurse Martin laughed again causing her leg to wiggle slightly. I saw her wince and cautioned her to remain still.

"My turn now," I said, urging her to sit back against the wall. "You won't believe the day I've had today. I'm not saying this is funny, but I do find it remarkable."

For the next several minutes I did my best to describe the happenings on our plane, embellishing only slightly here and there to add a little additional spice, not that it really needed any. When I finished, I slapped my forehead. "And now look at me! Here I am. What are the odds this happens, too? If I were you, once we're out of here, I'd get away from me as fast as you can. Who knows what else is in store tonight."

Both laughed, but nervously. "I think I agree with you," Dr. Symington said. "Sounds like very sound advice to me. You agree, Nurse Martin?"

Before she could respond, our attention was drawn to a bright light shining through the debris at the entrance, followed by the sounds of men clearing the area. Another voice called in, "We're secure out here. You're next. Be there straight away. Keep back. Keep clear."

It took about fifteen minutes for them to create an opening big enough for two men to squeeze in to check on us. One of the men was our co-pilot, who smiled broadly when he saw I wasn't hurt.

"Just making sure," he said, reaching down to take my

hand. "My job's to keep you safe, remember? You're precious cargo. Can't let anything happen to you."

"You're too kind," I said, standing and, without thinking, hugged him tightly. I immediately stepped back, and he laughed and shook his head.

"I guess anything would look good to you after this," he said, motioning around the hallway. "Even me."

"Even you," I said, smiling.

Dr. Symington nodded politely toward him before addressing the other man, a British sergeant. "That won't do," he said, pointing toward the entrance. "We'll need a stretcher in here for Nurse Martin. We'll sit tight while you widen the opening. And please call together some men to help do the carrying."

"Right so," the sergeant replied, saluting him smartly.

"I'll go with him," my co-pilot said. "Now don't you go anywhere in the meantime, you hear?"

I smiled and shooed him away. Dr. Symington just shook his head and said, "It's as I said before. You Yanks have a very *odd* sense of humor."

"I'm starting to believe you're right," I said, laughing again.

Nurse Martin added, "Why, I believe that man's sweet on you. Saw it in his eyes."

"No, now *you're* the one being funny," I replied. Still, just the thought she might have been on to something made me smile, which was another welcome distraction from the destruction at the end of the hall.

~

Sergeant Rigazzi was waiting for me when we were finally able to get Nurse Martin through the opening, which had been hastily braced up with long, thick boards, something one would expect to see in a mine shaft and not in a hospital. Still, this did the job, and we were finally free. The stretcher bearers moved her swiftly down the main hallway, Dr. Symington close behind. I called after him, "Would you like a hand?"

"Thank you, but no," he replied. "You have your own to take care of. I'll be by to check on them when I'm able." A few moments later they disappeared into a room down the hall.

Sam stepped forward and said, "Patients all settled in—down the other corridor over there. This place is like a maze, but, luckily, we were able to keep them all together in one of the larger ward rooms. Got them some sandwiches, too. They were starved. Everybody ate something. Do you want to see them now? They've been asking for you. Well, all except for Corporal Ernst. Even in all the excitement, he hasn't uttered a peep. Still, I can tell he knows what's going on, and I know he'd also like to know you're all right."

"They've had it rough today. Better look in on 'em. Please, lead the way, Sam."

As we made our way down the hallway, I was glad to see an armed guard had been posted outside the room. "Extra security for tonight," Sam explained. "Same all over the hospital. A corporal I ran into said more sabotage could be on the way soon. Hope it isn't until we get out of here, as bad as that sounds." I knew what he meant and couldn't have agreed more.

All but Corporal Ernst applauded when I entered the ward, and this was followed by a high, prolonged whistle by Private Montague. "Thanks, boys," I said, bowing slightly. "Shouldn't have worried. This sort of thing happens to me all the time." Sam just shook his head and smiled.

"So, let's see what we have, what we need to attend to tonight. Sergeant Rigazzi and I will start over here with Lieutenant Collins and work around to the rest of you. So, if you'll hold your horses, we'll get to you quick as we can. Finish your sandwiches, too. Might be some time before we eat again."

The first order of business was making sure the catheters were functioning properly and emptying the waste bags for Collins and Montague. I instructed Sam to make a note on his clipboard that these were to be checked right away at each stop. Private Montague also complained the bed sores on his back were starting to bite, so we cleaned him up, applied some medicated ointment, and rebandaged him. The sores had obviously been oozing pus all day, so I sincerely doubted we did much to alleviate his pain.

We also changed Captain Goldman's mask. Patients with active tuberculosis were required to wear a modified version of a surgical mask at all times to help protect others from catching the illness. Without such a mask, a sudden, wet cough had the potential to infect anyone in close range. He wasn't exactly complaining, but he did say he felt the mask made it more difficult at times to breathe, especially when lying down. I didn't tell him it likely wasn't the mask that was the culprit here; it was continued loss of function of his lungs at the root of that problem. I had Sam note that Captain Goldman should be kept upright as much as possible. A check of his temperature revealed a fever of 101, not uncommon for those at his stage of the illness. Still, I had him swallow two aspirin tablets to see if we could lower it some. I hated to admit it, but that was all we could do for him.

Corporal Ernst sat quietly on his bed and stared at the wall. While checking his pulse, I asked him how he was feeling. He looked at me, then back to the wall, all without uttering a sound. I patted him on the arm and said, "We'll be home soon. You hang in there."

Private Scalini was last, and he was really wound up. "Lieutenant, respectfully, you're one of the nicest looking officers I've ever seen."

"Why thank you, Tony," I said, "but my chart says you're having some pretty tough vision problems right now. That correct?"

"Exactly," he said, breaking into laughter. "That's why everybody looks so good to me!"

"Very funny, Soldier," I replied. "You better be careful or you'll end up with a nice shot with a long, rusty needle right in your rump before you hit the hay tonight. They say you never see the one that gets you, and in your case, with your eyes, that applies double, right?"

"Wow—gives it back as good as she receives it," he said, lying back. "I know when to put a lid on it."

"Good," I said, leaning down to place a cool compress over his eyes. "Keep that on there until you don't feel the cold any more. That will help with the pressure."

When we were finished, I turned to Sam and said, "Let's go update the charts." Looking back one more time, I said, "Men, we're going to go check on the plane. Hopefully, we'll be on schedule in the morning, so get all the rest you can. That's an order. Lights out now."

Lieutenant Collins raised himself slightly and said, "Thanks, Lieutenant. Thanks for everything."

"I appreciate it, but don't thank me yet. We're just starting and still have a long way to go. Tomorrow should go much smoother than today. At least let's hope so."

We turned off the lights and left the room.

∼

Once we were out in the main hallway, I asked Sam, "Our co-pilot asked us to meet them in the mess tent. Any idea where that is?"

"It's where I rounded up the sandwiches. I'm for that. I got them food, but I forgot to get something for myself. I could eat a horse about now."

"I'm right there with you. Stomach's been grumbling all day. Especially after, well, you know. So, you just show the way."

The crew was waiting for us and stood as we walked in. Except for our group and one attendant at a long table at the back, the place was deserted, which made sense for this time of night.

"Here comes Boom Boom!" the pilot shouted as he pulled out a chair and motioned me to sit down. "Now please don't take offense, but we've decided on a nickname for you."

As I sat down, he dramatically pushed in my chair and placed a napkin on my lap before continuing, "At first we were going to call you 'General' because we were told to do anything you asked of us, within reason of course, for the duration. But, we decided that might be too rough, especially after we saw you didn't look like the old crow who took care of Lieutenant Dix over there when he needed work on his wrist."

Here he paused, looked over at Sam, and said in a stage whisper, "Hurt it shootin' craps. I swear he did."

He turned back to me. "No, with your looks, we thought 'Princess' might be right, also given that you seem to be in charge of us right now. However, after what you've been through today, and especially after we saw you lose your chow, we finally decided on a nickname we think is going to be perfectly fitting: Boom Boom. Seems like everywhere you go there's a boom of some kind. Yeah, It'll fit."

Everyone laughed and saluted me. "Gentlemen, I'm not upset," I said, straightening my napkin and placing silverware in order in front of me. "To the contrary, I'm flattered. Never had a nickname before. I'll take it. Seems about right to me, too."

They laughed again, this time walking over to shake my hand and say, "Welcome, Boom Boom."

When they had finished, I realized something. "Wait a minute," I said, pointing at each of them. "I don't even know your names. There wasn't time at Karachi before we took off. I just know your stations, and that's not fair. Now it's your turn. And I want more than your name, rank, and serial number. I want to know something about you because, well, frankly, it looks like my life, and this poor stomach, are in your hands once we're off the ground."

I pointed to the pilot and said, "Let's start with you, the demolition derby driver. Maybe I should call you *Demolition Derby* after today's flight. Or maybe just 'DD' for short. What do you say about that?"

"Why, that wasn't a rough ride," he said, waving his hand side to side. "Had it all the way. Were you worried?"

All laughed as he continued. "I'm Paul Jordan—from Chicago. I was flying civilians here and there for Transcontinental & Western Air back home when I got the call. Mostly just short hops, but I loved it. Good money, saw lots of the country. Now I'm flying over the Hump and giving taxi rides to nurses. And, right now, I'm at your service. That's my story."

The co-pilot shot in, "And his nickname's 'Red.' After today, I think you've earned the right to call him that."

"Why 'Red'? I asked, confused. "His hair is so blonde it's almost white. What gives?"

"That's actually short for Rhode Island Red, the cockiest rooster in the barnyard," the co-pilot continued. "You see, Red here has a nurse at every stop we make, sometimes two. That's how he got his nickname."

"And are his missions always successful?" I teased.

He quickly added before Lieutenant Jordan could say anything in rebuttal, "Mostly, unless you count that nurse in Bombay a couple weeks back. Shot him down in flames. Oh, I could tell you a story . . . "

"That's enough of that," Lieutenant Jordan cut in. He turned to me. "Now I get to introduce you to him. Seems only fair."

Right at that moment the attendant walked toward us with a tray of sandwiches and glasses of milk. Once those had been passed around and we started eating, Lieutenant Jordan continued.

"This is Chuck Dunning. Says he's from Minneapolis, but who'd really admit to that? He was a jockey for cargo planes from the States up through Canada before the war. He swears it was mostly medicine and food goods for some pretty big companies, but it was probably contraband if the truth be known."

Lieutenant Dunning recoiled in mock horror as the description continued, "Doesn't chase skirts, so I don't trust him

much. Spends all his free time reading. Reading! He always has a
book or magazine stuck in his shirt. Never seen anything like it.
Reading! That's why his nickname is 'Books.' 'Books' Dunning."
"You might try it once yourself," Lieutenant Dunning
retorted, "If you ever actually learn to read."

When he looked over at me, I took my first really good
look at him. His face was strong with an angular jaw and pierc-
ing blue eyes. A pencil-thin mustache and two black curls that
sprung down his forehead were perfect compliments to his
tan complexion. His shoulders were also broad, and his torso
perfectly proportioned. "Movie star handsome," I thought to
myself.

We all laughed again as Lieutenant Dunning went on,
"So now it looks like I get to tell you about this guy, Lieutenant
Wilbur Dix of Raleigh, North Carolina. And if I hear one more
time how that's 'God's Country' I'm going to strangle him. To
hear him tell it, he was running a radio station there when his
call came. But, let's be honest here. His dad owns the station, so
we know how he got the job. The Army must have heard him
exaggerating about himself over the airwaves and figured he'd fit
in. Boy were they wrong. He's our radio operator and our navigator, although I have to tell you, I don't think he could find a
pitchfork in a haystack—or water if he fell out of a boat. Why,
he got us so lost last . . . "

"I didn't get us lost!" Lieutenant Dix interrupted, smiling
broadly and pointing a finger at both of them. "It was you two
knoteheads. I give the headings and course, but if you fall asleep
at the wheel from too much chicken chasing or somebody has
his nose in a magazine, no wonder we get off course. Not my
fault."

"And *his* nickname?" I asked.

Both, in unison, shouted, "Magellan! Because he never would have found his way around the globe if Dix here had been there with him. We'd still think the world is flat."

"You guys are very funny," he said, rolling his eyes. When the laughter subsided, Lieutenant Dix turned to me and said, "Wait a minute, we've a couple more to hear from. How about you, Nurse Ott. What's your background?"

All inched their chairs closer and purposely cleared their throats and straightened their ties while waiting for me to begin. "Not much to tell, really," I said, picking up my fork and pretended to polish it with my napkin. "I'm a New York girl. From Queens. Oh, I guess my claim to fame is I once had the record for holding my breath under water at our local swimming pool. Hard to top that, right?"

"You're playing with us," Lieutenant Dunning said. "Not fair. We want to know about you. Give!"

"Again, not much to say. Typical nurse story. Graduated college. Then nurse training. When the war broke out, we were badly needed, so I signed on like all of you. I want to do my part. That's my life, *really*."

"You're holding back," Lieutenant Dunning said, frowning. "There's more than that. You must be really important or have the goods on a high-ranking general somewhere. Or one of those patients you're transporting is Roosevelt in disguise. Has to be something like that, and I hope you soon trust us enough to fill us in. But, for now, we'll let you off the hook—only because you've already earned a nickname. Boom Boom. Somehow that fits you well."

"Thanks very much," I said, slapping him with my napkin. "Don't know how much I appreciate it."

I looked over and saw Sergeant Rigazzi, head down, staring at the floor. "We've one more, you know. This man here. Sam, tell us about yourself."

His face lit up as he addressed us. "Sam Rigazzi, present and accounted for. Home's in St. Louis. My family has had a restaurant there in the Italian section for three generations. I cook. Uncle Sam must have heard about my cooking, which is why it was decided somewhere along the line I'd be a good medic and convoy truck driver."

We all laughed as he added, this time his voice lowering and his demeanor changing, "I figured I might as well sign up because business slowed down so much after the war started. When Italy joined up with Hitler, I guess too many thought we'd be poisoning them or something and stopped coming in. So, I figured I could do more over here—and here I am."

The mood had turned mighty somber, so I pointed to Lieutenant Jordon and asked, "So, what about a nickname for Sam? Everybody else now has one."

"Don't know him that well," Lieutenant Jordan replied. "So, he'll have to earn one, though we can give him a *temporary*. I'd say 'Cookie' because of his braggin' about his cooking. I think that'll do for now."

I nodded my head in agreement. So did Sam. "Now, just one more thing I want to know now. Put down that sandwich and tell me this. I noticed this morning the picture of a beautiful woman painted on the nose of your ship. I think the name was 'Able Mabel,' right? Who's Mabel? One of your girlfriends, Red? One of your successful missions?"

He didn't respond. Neither did the others. No smiles, no laughter, nothing. All simply looked away, then down at the ground. It was obvious I had stepped over some sort of line, so I said, softly, "Sorry. I didn't mean to . . . "

After drinking down the last of his milk, Lieutenant Jordan finally spoke. "Getting late. Story for another night. We've much to do to get ready for the morning."

Lieutenant Jordan motioned for the attendant to come clear away our plates. "There are a couple of things I still need to share with you. No big damage today. We were lucky. The Brit ground crew is working on the gas line—that's all it was—and they'll have us ready to go by first light. We'll have take off at zero six thirty. Means we won't get much sack time tonight, but we've no choice. Too many miles to make tomorrow."

His face turned dead serious. "I want you to know tomorrow's a chute day. Parachutes will be put out for you and the others before you get aboard. The Germans are making one last-ditch effort to hang on close to the route we'll be taking. Might see some of the *Luftwaffe*. Hope not, but it could happen. That's why the chutes."

I interrupted him, "But I don't know anything about them. I wouldn't even know how to put one on."

He didn't respond. Instead, he continued, "We don't have any guns. No Red Cross markings on the ship. Nothing to indicate we're hauling wounded. I thought it my duty to mention this."

"If you're trying to scare me, you've done a pretty good job."

"Not trying to scare you," he said, his face softening. "Just stating the facts I'd want to know if I were in your shoes."

Looking at his watch, he said, "Time to turn in. We better get what little rest we can. Especially you, Boom Boom. Tomorrow's going to be a long day."

The others smiled and nodded their agreement.

I stood and studied their faces, They were all going to be right.

∼

Chapter 5

Moments of Relief

0612 ZULU, January 18
British General Hospital
Aden, Saudi Arabia

LIEUTENANT JORDAN HADN'T BEEN KIDDING when he said morning would come early. I had to roust everyone at zero five hundred to have barely enough time to get all back to the ship and settled in before we were scheduled for takeoff. I felt like I had just closed my eyes when the alarm clock started ringing. I didn't even have time for a quick sponge bath. I slipped on my uniform, quickly brushed my hair, dabbed a thin layer of lipstick, put on my hat, and met the day looking, I was sure, like something the cat dragged in. My mind was still foggy, but I knew I had to shake that at once. Pouring a large cup of coffee, I gulped as much as I could. It didn't help.

Two armed sentries met us at the plane and checked our tags before letting us aboard. The crew wasn't inside, but obviously they had been there quite a bit earlier, as evidenced by the parachutes waiting for us. Just looking at them frightened me, so I slid them out of sight under the seats and litters.

There was no time for a regular breakfast, so Sam and I

improvised the best we could. I managed to round up a large jug of hot coffee while he talked the cooks into a couple sacks of biscuits and a few slices of ham. At least we had enough for a quick bite to eat before departure.

In addition to the food, Sam had somehow procured for us badly needed medical supplies. He wouldn't tell me how he got them, but now we were flush with cotton, bandages, iodine, quinine, and two large bottles of aspirin tablets. He also managed ten blankets, which I knew we'd need if we reached higher altitudes. We had been provided very little in the way of medicines before leaving Karachi, so this felt like Christmas morning to me. The icing on the cake was a bottle of brandy, which he handed me saying, "For medicinal purposes only, of course."

"There's a word for people like you," I said, shaking my head and pretending disapproval.

"Scrounger?"

"That wasn't the word I had in mind, but that probably should be your new nickname."

"I think I'm more of a liberator. How about that instead?"

We both laughed as Sam set off to accomplish one more "liberation" before we had to take off. I thought it best I didn't know where he was going in case I was asked questions later.

After he had gone, I scraped the label off one of the bottles of aspirin tablets so its contents couldn't be identified. One of the senior nurses in my last training program had taught us all a valuable trick. I made sure none of my charges was looking as I removed all the tablets and ground them up finely in a large coffee cup. I poured the powder back inside the bottle. Ground up aspirin could be sold as anything to patients, especially nervous ones. Pain reducer, nerve settler, bowel savior, grip chaser. Then, making sure all of them *did* see what I was doing, I spooned a little into cups of water and passed them around. "Men, this is special medicine to prevent flight nausea," I said as seriously as I could muster. After what they had been through yesterday, they all gratefully gulped it down. However, I had my suspicions Captain Goldman had either seen me in action or had done the same in the past with his dental patients. He winked as I handed him his cup, but he also drank it down, smacking his lips loudly, setting an example for the others. I winked back.

The crew finally showed up just a few minutes before our scheduled takeoff. After they had climbed in, each took the time to visit briefly with our patients, which I thought was pretty wonderful. They gave a quick status update and assured us the British ground crew had done a "smashing" job of making repairs to the gas line. That news earned a light round of applause. As Lieutenants Jordan and Dix made their way up the aisle to the cockpit, Lieutenant Dunning stayed behind to ask if there was anything he could do to help out. I could tell by his voice he was sincere, that he really did care about our welfare. I thanked him and assured him I'd call out if I needed anything. With that, he saluted, turned, and went to his seat.

After he had gone, Sam turned to me and said, "Let me see—was he asking about the patients or you? He sure looks at you funny. Better watch that boy if you know what's good for you."

"Why, whatever do you mean?" I replied. "He's just a nice man is all."

"Yeah, a nice man who might have his sights set on somebody I know. Mark my words."

The teasing stopped when Lieutenant Dunning swung around in his chair and called back to us, "Initiating takeoff. Hold tight!"

What I knew about aviation could be put in a thimble, but as the engines began to roar, they sounded good. They must have been functioning well because it was only a short distance down the strip before we were off the ground and headed steadily upward. My first takeoff the previous morning had made me feel so queasy I had to search for a bucket. Not so this time. I still wasn't wild about having my feet off the ground, but at least this time my first thoughts in the air were of my patients, who all seemed to be doing nicely. Even Lieutenant Collins and Private Montague, the litter-bound, seemed calm as they were rocked gently back and forth.

As soon as we had stopped our climb and leveled off, the realization came to me as if in a flash bulletin. Too much coffee. I had to go to the bathroom. This had not been an issue the day before because our refueling stops had been timely, but I knew we had over four hours to go before our first one. Sam saw me looking around and asked, "Need something? What can I do?"

"I don't know exactly how to put this," I said, matter-of-factly, "but if I don't find a way to get rid of some of my coffee . . ."

"Oh, this is going to be good," he said, laughing loudly.

I immediately shot back, "Not funny! Not at all!" It was also at that moment I realized all the others had heard me, too, and more laughter followed.

"Sorry, Lieutenant" he said, trying to stifle a broad smile. "No disrespect intended. It's just, well, the C-47 isn't exactly equipped with the necessities a woman might need. Designed definitely for men."

"So, what am I supposed to do? I can't be the first woman ever to be on one of these things."

"Well," he said, pointing back behind me. "See that little trough about three feet off the floor. The one with a hole at its rear. That's called the 'Relief Hole,' and that's what I use when nature calls."

The laughter became so loud Lieutenant Dunning came back to investigate. "What did I miss?" he asked, smiling.

"Nothing yet, but just you wait," Private Scalini called out, causing the laughter to become so loud the rest of the crew craned their necks to get a good look at us.

With my hands on my hips, I said, "This is barbaric, you know." Turning and pointing, I asked, "How in the world am I expected to use . . . use *that!*"

Private Scalini grinned. "With great accuracy, we hope!"

While some might have thought that funny, this time none laughed. He had stepped over the line some, and the others knew it. Still, I didn't scold him. There wasn't time. I was concerned about a solution, first and foremost.

Lieutenant Dunning came to my rescue, and I could have kissed him right on the spot for doing so. "Look, we've had women on board before. The solution is simple, if some chivalry is used. Any blankets around here?"

Sam pointed to the pile he had "liberated" earlier. "Will these do?"

Lieutenant Dunning grabbed one, shook it out, and held it up. "One man holds up this end, and another takes the other side. Both do an about-face and keep eyes front while duty is performed. Easy as pie."

"But there's no way on this earth . . ." I protested, pointing again behind me.

Without saying anything, Lieutenant Dunning picked up a large cup from a tray attached to the wall and handed it to me. "I'll let you figure out the rest." He smiled and headed back up the aisle.

Sam said, "Scalini, you take this end. I'll do the other. Keep your eyes toward the cockpit, or I'll personally shove you out that cargo door. My meaning clear?"

"Yes, Sergeant," he replied in a tone of voice that suggested he also knew earlier he had gone too far.

What followed was a challenge—but also a success. And, just another first. I guessed there would be many more along our way.

∼

After four hours and forty-two minutes, we reached our first refueling stop, exactly as scheduled, at Gura, Ethiopia. After we had taxied to the refueling trucks, Lieutenant Jordan walked back to us.

"Look, you're not going to have many orders from me, but I'm giving you one now," he said, as serious as I'd seen him carry himself. "All eyes on me."

He explained we were not to leave the ship, no matter how stiff we felt. The city of Gura was, he said, essentially gone—demolished. Virtually all the homes, businesses, and places of worship had been leveled by the Italians to make room for a military base and airfield. Until only a few months before, the whole area had been under the control of the Italian Air Force to serve as their main base of operation to support the Axis takeover of North Africa. They had finally been routed and driven out, but they also wanted the area back so badly they were still regularly sending groups of fighters and bombers to blast the area. What was left of the base was now under control of a small group of Australian soldiers who made sure the Allies received fuel and supplies when routed this direction.

"Nothing to see here," he said. "That is, nothing except the bravery of the men refueling us right now. I don't know how they do it. They get bombed. They dig out. Over and over and over. Must feel like ants after a hard rain destroys their nests. Tough as nails, all of 'em. I'm just glad they're on our side.

"We're leaving again as soon as the tanks are full. No visiting here. We need to be off the ground as fast as possible."

Lieutenant Jordan paused as he turned to leave. "I've also a favor to ask. For those of you who can, wave out the windows to these fellows as we taxi out. Would you do that for me?"

It couldn't have been more than ten minutes when we were back in the air and on the second leg of our route for the day—Khartoum, in the Egyptian Sudan. Once at our cruising altitude, Lieutenant Dunning made a quick visit and informed us that we had about three and a half hours before we'd be on the ground again. He also chatted briefly with all the patients before heading back to the cockpit.

"Nice fellow, don't you think?" Sam said. "Would make someone a good catch one of these days. I'm just saying."

"I know what you're saying," I said, giving it right back. "But right now, all I want is to get back home. One day down. Six more to go. And, they go by fast enough for me."

Sam nodded. "Couldn't agree more with you there."

We soon settled into a relatively smooth, bump-free flight—a great comfort to all of us. I didn't exactly feel like I was gaining what Lieutenant Dunning had described as "air legs," but at least all trace of nausea was finally gone. I took that as a moral victory and a satisfying accomplishment for my second day of flying.

I also built up enough courage to unbuckle myself from my seat and regularly check on my patients. All seemed fine except Private Montague. He said he had significant pain radiating from the bedsores up near his shoulder blades. It would have been too difficult to change the bandages in flight, so I excused myself and went back to my medical bag. I kept the aspirin bottle inside and out of view while I unscrewed the cap and shook out two tablets. I filled a cup with water, went back to him, and said, "These pain pills will help. They'll give you relief until we clean you up tonight. Swallow them whole—no chewing—and see if you can sleep a little. They'll probably make you drowsy."

Sam leaned over and said to him, "Do as she says. You'll feel better in no time."

On the way back to my seat, Sam stopped me. "Thank you," he said.

"No," I replied. "Thank you."

Before we knew it, Lieutenant Dix walked halfway back toward us and announced, "Khartoum just ahead. Tighten everything down. This strip's been known to have a hole or two. Don't worry—just be ready."

His words were prophetic. Right after touchdown, we bounced roughly several times, once so hard my knee was slammed sideways to the wall, followed by the sound of a rip in the hem of my skirt. At least the rip distracted me from the knot that immediately started forming on my kneecap.

Once we had stopped, I stood and looked out the window. No base was there, just the landing strip and a supply depot run by a small group of British soldiers. I asked where the city was, and Lieutenant Dunning pointed off in the distance and said, "About four miles to the west. Way over there. Put the strip this far out for security reasons. Smart move. I'd have done the same."

I noticed how the wind lifted sand and swirled it everywhere creating what looked like miniature tornadoes. With those conditions present, we thought it best to keep our patients on board.

The crew finally stepped out to check over the plane and visit with our hosts. After making sure all had come through the landing in good order, Sam and I also climbed down to stretch our legs and see what we could do about getting some food. Thankfully, the British ground crew had just prepared their lunch.

In a lovely British voice, the oldest member of the crew said, while pointing to their small mess tent, "Please, help yourselves. Just want you chaps to know how much we appreciate what you're doing. Get all you need."

Here he paused, moved closer to us, locked his hands together, and added, "We're strong together. So strong that paperhanger won't be able to keep us out of his knickers for long. I'll bet a pound or two on that any day."

Even I got the reference to Hitler, and we all laughed and shook hands. The camaraderie and solidarity felt good.

The Brits gave us enough sandwiches and coffee for all aboard the *Able Mabel,* an act of kindness I knew I'd not soon forget. After saying our goodbyes, we were about to go back inside when a group of six planes in tight formation and at low altitude screamed overhead, startling us all, as they headed west. All the British soldiers stopped what they were doing, raised their hands, and loudly urged on what were obviously their countrymen. "Going to join Monty!" one of them called out. Another added, "They'll have the rest of the Jerrys on the run straight away! Won't be long now!" The pride in their voices was so strong it made me shiver.

"Those were Hurricanes," Sam said. "Going somewhere in one heck of a hurry. Best they've got. Great pilots, too. I hope they really give it to 'em. Right in the kisser!"

I looked up and saluted them myself. "Godspeed, boys. And be safe."

Sam and I had just returned to our seats when the engines started and we rolled down the strip. The whole stop had taken just over fifteen minutes. This time I hardly paid any attention to the liftoff as I kept watch on the litters to make sure they didn't sway too much side to side. Sam must have noticed, and said, "Appears you're a real veteran now. I'm starting to get pretty proud of you."

"Thanks. I'm trying. I don't know if I'll ever get completely used to all this, but at least I wasn't looking for another bucket."

We both laughed, and it felt good.

∾

Lieutenant Dunning, as he had after our first stop of the day, came back to visit with us as soon as we leveled off. Right next to me was what Sam called a "fold-down-from-the-wall, flop seat" we weren't using. Lieutenant Dunning lowered it and sat down, accidentally stepping on my foot in the process. I yelped and jerked my leg back.

"I'm so sorry!" he said, standing again, which caused the seat to snap back up. As he shifted his weight, he caught my foot again. "Oh, no! Please forgive me. I'm all feet today."

"Well, I'll forgive you. That is, I will if you'll keep those clodhoppers away from me from now on."

"Deal," he said, laughing and sitting again, this time making sure he kept a safe distance. He pointed to the coffee jug and asked, "OK?" I nodded it was, and as he poured himself a cup, he said, "We've about four hours before El Fasher, so I thought we could visit a while, if you don't mind. I've just got to ask you something. I've been thinking and thinking about this, and I just can't figure it out. Lieutenant, just why are we hauling you? It's driving me crazy."

When he stopped for a couple of sips, I said, "To be perfectly honest, I'm not quite sure myself. Oh, I was given some rigmarole before we started, but I can't really talk about. All I can say, and I'm sure you know this, is we have to be back stateside in a week, a little less than that now."

"One of you has to be a spy, right?" he asked, pushing his hat back. "Saw something that will help shorten the war? One of these men an aid to Patton? Come on, you've got to give me something."

I looked around and motioned him to lean closer. "OK, I'll tell you—if you promise to keep a secret. Can you do that?"

He excitedly rubbed his hands together and leaned in. When our faces were just about touching, I whispered, again first glancing around, "I am a spy. Bringing back something top secret. Want to know what it is?"

His face grew completely serious as he nodded rapidly. "Well, I snuck into Germany and got . . ."

I stopped, moved my lips until they touched his left ear. "I got a map of . . ."

"Yes, yes!" he said. "Go on."

"A map of . . . the sauerkraut factory in Berlin!"

He started to applaud but stopped short when he realized he'd been had. "You're so funny," he said, losing his grip on his cup and spilling half of the coffee right on my shoes. This time I stood up and kicked my feet to shake off the liquid.

"You did that on purpose!" I said, swatting him on the shoulder.

"It wasn't on purpose—I swear. But I couldn't be blamed if it had been. You're terrible. Had me going all the way."

He was scolding me, but his smile told me another story. It also did for Sam, who had heard the whole conversation. "If you two don't break it up," he said, handing me a towel to dry my shoes, "people are going to start talking."

"Why, I . . . I . . ." Lieutenant Dunning stammered. "I need to get back to work." He handed me the coffee cup and marched quickly back up the aisle. He didn't look back.

"You better watch it," Sam said, looking up at me. "He's crazy about you. I see that for sure now. Going to follow you around like a dog unless you do something about it. I'm just saying."

"Oh, he's not that interested in me," I said, slipping one shoe back on. "I imagine he's just bored and looking for someone new to talk about."

"Yeah, right. And I'm the Queen of Sheba."

As I looked up at the cockpit, I was starting to hope he was right.

∾

We settled into a very smooth flight, so much so that after Sam and I had checked over our patients once again and updated their charts, we were each able to nap for almost two hours. The steady drone of the engines actually started to be quite soothing, and I fell into a sleep so deep I started dreaming about being back in nursing school, about the day I graduated. However, the dream started fading just as I was handed my diploma.

Sam and I were jolted awake when the plane suddenly banked hard left, which caused several cups and plates to crash to the floor right at his boots. We looked at each other. He didn't speak, but I could see the concern in his eyes. Still half asleep, I looked at my watch and did a quick calculation. I figured we were at best about two hours from El Fasher. I started to mention this to Sam when we banked even steeper.

"Not again," I said while blowing out a breath. "More engine trouble you think?"

"Don't think so." He jumped up and made his way to the nearest window. As he did, I looked first to our patients, all of whom were now wide awake and looking at me as if waiting for an explanation. I didn't say anything, which seemed to make them only more scared. I looked toward the cockpit. I could barely make it out, but I was quite sure I heard what Lieutenant Dunning was saying to the others.

"Two o'clock high now. He's seen us. Sure of it. Still— could be ours."

After a few moments, and as we continued to bank downward, he shouted, "Messerschmitt!"

≈

Chapter 6

Forget the Parachutes

1416 ZULU, January 18
(125 miles northeast of El Fasher, Egyptian Sudan)

WE CONTINUED BANKING SO SEVERELY to the left that soon
the sun was shining in the opposite windows, indicating we had
done almost a complete about-face. Just as suddenly, the right
wing dipped down as we began a dive that direction. The engines
roared louder than I had ever heard them, fading off only when
my ears closed up tight, making everything sound off in a long
tunnel.

On his knees, Sam struggled to keep Lieutenant Collins in
his stretcher. Private Scalini crawled over to help him, the bandage on his head falling off as he did so. Once able to move, I
grabbed hand holds along the wall and made my way to Private
Montague, who was pressing against his ribs, clenching his teeth,
and wincing in pain. The straps holding him to the stretcher had
loosened, and the force and angle of the dive had pinned him to
the wall.

Just as I reached him, our direction changed again, violently throwing us all back left. Catching my skirt on the edge of
a stretcher, I lost my balance and went down hard, my shoulder

smashing against a group of bolts clustered on the floor. A sharp, burning tingle shot down my arm as I tried righting myself again.

Then, the oddest thing happened. Over the shrill roar of the engines, I heard two high-pitched whooshes that reminded me of Fourth of July fireworks rockets just taking off skyward. When I turned around to look that direction, I saw two large holes in the roof of the plane about half way up the aisle. Thin rays of sunshine passed through them, the end points of which dragged small golden circles in a jagged path across the floor as our banking continued.

"We've been hit!" Lieutenant Dix shouted from the cockpit. "I'll check damage!"

None of us uttered a sound.

Lieutenant Dix flung off his headset, moved as quickly as he could back toward us, and looked up to examine the holes. Turning to me, he asked, "Anyone hurt?"

"No," was all I could say, still trying to steady myself.

Without another word, he clawed himself back behind the cockpit and said something I couldn't catch to Lieutenant Jordan.

As soon as he was seated, we banked again hard right, to the point we were all almost on our sides. I didn't see how he made it back to us, but when I looked up again, Lieutenant Dunning was before me, clutching desperately at a hook above his head.

He seemed almost out of breath, his words coming in short bursts. "We can't outrun him. So, we'll just have to outmaneuver. He's far out, so likely low on fuel. Can't stay with us long. At least we hope so.

"Got one thing to try. You need to know about it—to keep

everyone secure. Last October at El Alamein, our pilots flew out wounded—but kept getting shot down. No markings for them to see. Rommel didn't approve the killing of wounded. Let it be known we should flap wings fast, side to side to show wounded inside. We're going to try it. Don't know if it'll work, but we have to try. Brace everyone. Now. And hold on."

As he was about to turn, I asked, "What about the parachutes?"

He looked directly at me and said quietly, so the others wouldn't hear, "Forget the parachutes." He shook his head and walked toward the cockpit.

Once Lieutenant Dunning was back in his seat, Lieutenant Jordan first leveled off again and then immediately dipped the wings deeply and dramatically side to side. I didn't look down to see what it was, but objects once again rolled back and forth under our feet, crashing into one side, then back to the other. All the while, Sam and I did our best to hold the stretchers to their moorings. Private Scalini timed it so when the plane dipped left he was able to scoot over to help Sam. Just behind me, Captain Goldman said through his mask, "Can I help you? Anything I can do?"

"If you can, reach forward and press against my hips. Try to keep me up. I'm slipping."

That helped. I turned and nodded my thanks. As I did so, I saw Corporal Ernst had also stood, grabbed an anchor, and used his other arm to support Captain Goldman.

We kept flapping, the dips seeming to go deeper and deeper each time. Suddenly, I heard the screaming of engines as a large shadow swept across our windows, first on the right, then the left.

A few moments later, the dipping slowed and became more shallow until we fell into a gentle swaying back and forth.

"There he is!" Sam called out, pointing through the left bank of windows. He was visible only during the rise from a left side dip, but there was the *Messerschmitt,* now flying parallel to us. The pilot dipped his wings quickly four times—then banked out of sight.

∾

While Sam and I attended to our patients, all of whom had come through remarkably well, Lieutenant Dunning walked back to inspect the damage. He first examined the holes at the top of the ship, then knelt and felt around on the floor. I could see his eyes light up as he said, to no one in particular, "Lucky. Luck of the Irish."

He had found the matching holes for the ones in the ceiling and got down on his stomach to poke his fingers in and investigate further. After a few moments, he stood back up and called to the cockpit, "Through and through. Doesn't appear too bad. Looks like it missed everything that could have taken us down."

Turning to me, he said while shaking his head, "A few feet either way and . . ."

He didn't have to finish the thought. His meaning was clear. In response, I blew a kiss and said, "I never thought I'd thank a German for anything. But, that's for you, General Rommel. Thank you—for our lives."

"I'm glad you're OK," he said, stepping forward and taking my hands.

I squeezed his hands, tightly, and replied, "Thanks, Chuck. You, too."

"I better get back," he said. "We're not out of the woods yet."

When he had gone, I turned back to Sam, who was grinning broadly.

"Don't you say a word!" I said, shaking a finger at him. "Not one."

He raised a hand and made the motion of zipping his lips.

It took us the better part of an hour to clean up our part of the ship. This time it wasn't just ration cans that had scattered around. Everything, from our medical supplies to dishes to our apparently useless parachutes, had found new homes. Putting everything back to proper storage was useful, though, as it gave us the opportunity to take a complete inventory. When that was completed, Sam said he'd make a point of liberating some additional supplies at our next stop to fill a few needs and supplement what we already had. I now knew what he meant by "liberating," and I was perfectly fine with that.

After we had finished policing the area and checking on our patients again, Sam motioned to our chairs and suggested we settle back a few minutes to relax. However, my mind was still racing. I just couldn't get something straight.

"Sam, why'd he do it?" I asked, looking out the window.

"Well, it's like the Lieutenant said. He was taking a long-shot, but it had worked before at El Alamein. Jordan's a pretty smart guy if you ask me. He's OK."

"No . . . not him. I'm talking about the German pilot. Why'd he let us go? He could see plain as day we were the enemy. He could have shot us down, and nobody would have ever known he'd done it. So, he didn't need to do what he did. He could just as easily have killed us all and flown back to his base.

With patients or no patients, we're still his enemy. And some patients get well and go back to fight—to kill another day. He knows that. So, why didn't he finish us? I just don't understand at all."

Sam looked through the window ahead of us. "I figure he must have been through the earlier battles and heard about what the wing motion meant. Must have been with Rommel."

"But he was German," I said. "Look what they're doing all over Europe. I don't recall any acts of kindness or compassion with any of that, do you? Think of all the people they've already killed—all the countries they've destroyed. I've always thought of them as nothing but monsters. It's us or them, right? There aren't any shades of gray here. None that make any sense. They're monsters—or . . ."

I didn't know how to finish saying what I was thinking. I felt so confused, yet so grateful at the same time for what had just happened—from an enemy.

"Look," Sam said, leaning closer, pulling a chain out from his uniform. Attached to it was a small, silver cross. He rubbed it between his fingers. "I've always believed there has to be some good, at least a tiny bit, in everyone. That's what my faith tells me."

He let the cross fall to his chest. "He wouldn't have been here if he hadn't survived the fight up north, and that was as bad as it gets—on both sides. That means he's seen death. Probably a lot of it. Maybe he's tired of the killing. Or, maybe he was making up in his own way for what he's done before. Guilt? Compassion? We'll never know what made him fly away. And maybe he won't ever, either. But I still say at the bottom of this there is good in him. We're lucky that showed through today."

Sam looked over as if expecting me to reply, but I didn't. My thoughts were still too unsettled.

We sat there quietly for a few minutes, wrapped in our own thoughts, when Lieutenant Dix called back, "El Fasher dead ahead. Prepare for landing."

This time the strip was smooth as a billiard table. Sam made the sign of the cross and said, "Thank you, Lord." Looking at me, he smiled. "Don't think I could have taken one more bounce today."

"Me, either. I don't know about you, but I'm going to go kiss the ground right now."

"You just lead the way. I'll be right behind you."

≈

Chapter 7

No Firing Squad Today

1508 ZULU, January 18
El Fasher, Egyptian Sudan

OUR LANDING AT EL FASHER was just after fifteen hundred, which meant we had been travelling right at eleven hours, our visit with the *Messerschmitt* included. We were all exhausted but still had much to do before our heads could touch pillows.

When Sam flung open the cargo door, the heat blasted me. It felt about a hundred degrees, and when I complained to Sam, he said, "January is the hottest month over here. Not uncommon to be well over a hundred during the day. And dry. Very dry. Better drink lots of water while we're here. All of us."

I nodded. "I don't see any Brits or any of ours. Who's in charge here? Do you know?"

Startling me for an instant, Lieutenant Dix tapped me on the shoulder from behind and said, "These are the Sudanese. They took a good whacking from the Germans and Italians, and now they're mad as wet hornets—looking to get even. We couldn't ask for better allies, at least not in this part of the continent. Uncle Sam has offered to pay for everything they do for us, but they won't take a nickel. Too proud—and too much to prove I guess. Just tell 'em what you need, and I'm sure they'll pitch in straight away."

He smiled. "I've seen their hospital before. It is . . . *interesting.* At least I think you'll find it so."

"What do you mean?" I asked, my curiosity climbing. "What's so *interesting* about it?"

"Not saying another word. You'll find out." He tipped his cap and headed back up the aisle.

Sam said, "Everything's been *interesting* today. I'll take normal. That's all I want now."

Once we were outside the ship, the wind and heat slammed at my face. "You weren't kidding," I said, fanning myself. "Hot as blazes."

I hoped transport would be waiting for us, but other than the refueling trucks, no other vehicles were around. While the crew examined the ship, I walked over to ask Lieutenant Dunning what I should do.

When I got there, I saw he was stepping up on a small crate so he could reach high enough to examine the exit holes made by the bullets. "Still can't believe it. Looks like all we got was some additional ventilation. Couldn't be any luckier."

Finally noticing me standing there, he asked, "Something I can do for you?"

"Sorry to interrupt, but what can I do to get the men to the hospital?"

Pointing to the ground crew, he said, "Ask one of them. Most of the Sudanese speak at least a little English. If they can't help, let me know."

He turned back to the others, who were still looking up and shaking their heads. I walked over to the refueling truck and saw that a soldier I guessed no more than sixteen was sitting by himself in the cab while the others worked to get the plane ready.

"Excuse me," I said, tapping on the door. I startled him, and he immediately reached for a rifle on the seat next to him.

"I'm American!" I shouted, stepping back quickly. "American!"

Lieutenant Dunning heard me and came running over. "What's the problem here?" he asked, looking first at me, then at the soldier.

"I frightened him is all. He didn't see me come up."

The soldier only glanced at me before he addressed Lieutenant Dunning, "What, Sir? What you want?"

Both struggled for words that could be understood, and plenty of hand signs were thrown in for good measure. Finally, Lieutenant Dunning shook the soldier's hand and walked over to me.

"Looks like we'll have to take a walk," he said, pointing off in the distance. "Hospital's right over there. Not far. You can see it from here. Take a look. I'll take you over, and we'll get a truck back here right away."

"No, that's OK," I said. "I'll do it. It'll be good to stretch my legs. Don't mind a bit. You've a lot to do. I'll be fine."

"You sure?" he asked, looking back at the plane. "I can go with you if you want."

"Don't worry about me. I'll find the way. Please, you just make sure we can get along again tomorrow. We really have to, you know."

He smiled. "We'll be ready, Elsie. You can bank on that. Now, off with you. Get your work done. You have to be exhausted."

After he had gone, I told Sam what I was doing and headed toward the hospital. I could feel the heat of the sand through the soles of my shoes. Hot didn't even begin to describe this climate. *Brutal* was more like it. Sweat soon dripped down my forehead, and as I wiped it away, sand flying by stuck to it. In a matter of seconds, the area just above my eyes felt like sandpaper.

The hospital looked pretty ordinary to me, other than the fact it was all on one level. It was quite large, maybe as wide as the length of a football field. Every section had multiple, large windows, which I figured made sense given the heat, and all appeared to be open. Curtains were flapping everywhere, which made the building look positively alive. As I got closer, I noticed the hospital was made of some type of pinkish stone that resembled a combination of marble and granite.

I stepped through the main doors, and two guards greeted me. Thankfully, both spoke English fairly well. Once I let them know what I wanted, one said he'd go find a nurse and be right back. The other guard, a tall, dark-skinned man with a maroon beret covering most of his head, attempted making small talk, mostly about the weather. When it became obvious communication was going to be tough, we settled into the universal fanning of our faces and wiping our foreheads. In the end, we laughed, heartily, and then fell silent, both looking down the hallway and hoping the nurse would soon show up.

To our collective relief, she did. "I am Nurse Aya Nazari. And you?"

"Nurse Elsie Ott," I replied, extending my hand and shaking hers. "So pleased to meet you."

I guessed Nurse Nazari to be about twenty-five, and she was, in a word, beautiful. Her eyes were a deep brown, which paired nicely with her smooth, light-tan complexion. She was petite, just over five feet. Her hair was raven black, but the sheer scarf wrapped around the top of her head hid whether it was straight or curly.

When she let go of my hand, I thought to myself what a sight I must have appeared to her. I hadn't bathed in two days, my uniform was crumpled like an old newspaper, my hair was tangled and dry as straw, and my lipstick was only a memory.

I was going to make excuses when she said, "Sorry, we didn't expect you until tomorrow. That's what we were told."

Her English was also very good. "What doesn't she have going for her?" I thought to myself, realizing immediately this wasn't a time to be catty. Still, we looked like a princess and the Bride of Frankenstein.

"How many patients have you?"

"Five—and a medic with me as well. I'd appreciate it if we could get them here so I can attend to them. We've had a very long day, so just getting them off that plane will do them a world of good."

Without responding to me, she motioned for one of the guards to come over. She said a few words to him in their language, turned back to me and said, "All has been taken care of. If you'll please go with him, he'll see all are brought back here. I'll prepare a space."

"Thank you so much," I said, again shaking her hand. "This is wonderful of you."

She smiled. "We will be of service all we can. You are welcome."

I followed the guard out the door and to a large truck parked just to the right of the entrance. He opened the door for me, and I climbed in. Sam had everyone ready when we got back to the plane, so it didn't take much effort get everyone loaded up and on the way to the hospital. This time, Nurse Nazari and several orderlies rushed out to greet us.

"Just tell them what you want," Nurse Nazari said, pointing to the orderlies. "They'll take over now."

I thanked her and introduced Sam. After that, all we had to do was stand back and give the orders. Once inside and past the entrance area, I understood why Lieutenant Dix had described the place as *interesting.* The hallways were so narrow the stretchers literally scraped the walls as they were being carried. Complicating that, every dozen feet or so, the hallway either angled sharply right or left, almost like we were moving along a maze. Leading us through this maze, Nurse Nazari finally stopped and ordered everyone inside a room to her right.

The entrance seemed even narrower than the hall, so I didn't see any way they were going to get the stretchers in there. I was just about to caution them about the need to be gentle with those patients when, in perfectly orchestrated movements, other orderlies made their way by, moved in place, and pressed their chests firmly against the stretchers as these were tilted to the side. Neither Lieutenant Collins or Private Montague showed the least bit of discomfort while this took place. Much to my surprise, both were smiling. The orderlies kept the full weight of their bodies against them as the stretchers were rotated, allowing them to be taken in the room. Obviously, they had done this before. But, still, I was impressed.

The large room had enough examination tables for everyone. "OK, boys," I said, "We're going to give you a good going over. Our hosts have agreed to lend a hand, so we'll do this as fast as we can. I know you'd like to have a snack and get some shuteye. So would I. Let's get going."

As soon as I had gone over the charts with Nurse Nazari, she went around the room and assigned an orderly to each of our men. Another nurse showed up. Nurse Ganim was in charge of making sure all tasks were performed properly. All I had to do was stand back and watch, which was fine with me. The break felt good—and I needed it.

With the opportunity at hand, I asked Nurse Nazari why the building was constructed in this manner. She smiled and said, "Visitors always ask. This place over three hundred years old, possibly more. Once belong to a sheik and was his harem. Halls narrow in case of him attacked."

"Attacked? What do you mean?"

"Narrow makes easy to defend. Only one can move forward at a time. Not several. One man easy to stop. Many at same time difficult. When all family in one room, could fight off intruders. Understand now?"

"That's genius," I said. "Never thought of that. But, it wouldn't hurt to widen the halls just a little today. Would be a lot easier for everyone, don't you think?"

"We are used to it. Not a problem to us."

Based on what I had witnessed earlier, she was right.

As it turned out, all the orderlies were trained in basic medical care. They were also, as I soon discovered, quite good at it. With Nurse Ganim moving from table to table to assist if needed, they completed their tasks. One irrigated and rebandaged Private Montague's bedsores. Another applied a new dressing to Private Scalini's scalp wound. Two others, under the watchful eyes of Nurse Nazari and myself, replaced Lieutenant Collins' and Private Montague's catheters—and did so in excellent fashion. All were also given quick, but thorough sponge baths behind movable screens to allow for privacy, which I could tell the men appreciated.

The only one not given full care and attention was Captain Goldman. They just weren't quite sure what to do with him, and their anxiety was evident. I tried explaining as best I could the odds of catching tuberculosis from him were quite small, especially if masks were worn, but this didn't comfort them much. So, I stepped in and took over when needed. He understood and thanked our hosts the most of all.

After the medical care was completed, Nurse Nazari saw to it that trays of local fruits and breads were brought in and served. These were greatly appreciated and disappeared without a crumb left behind.

"I don't know how I . . . we can ever thank you enough for your kindness," I said, grasping both of Nurse Nazari's hands and squeezing them. "I'll never forget this."

"We are just very glad to help our friends," was her reply. "Thank you for what you are doing for us."

What she said next was sweet music to my ears. "Would you like to wash up yourself? It can be arranged. We have a room for our nurses here. Down the corridor a little farther. And, there are beds there, too, for the night for you—if you wish."

"Thank you, but first I must get back to our plane right away to see when the crew says we will be leaving tomorrow. Afterwards, yes, I'd be very grateful for the hospitality. I know I look a mess."

She shook her head as if to disagree with my assessment, but she also smiled, which told me I needed to do my best to get back to a wash basin and a brush.

~

The same guard who had driven us to the hospital took me back to the plane. When I stepped out of his truck, I noticed a small crowd gathered at the cargo door and went over to investigate.

As soon as I reached the outer ring of the group, which consisted of what appeared to be a dozen or so local citizens, I inched my way through and heard Lieutenant Jordan talking to an older, distinguished-looking man wearing a tight-fitting black suit and a bright red fez hat with a thick, gold tassel that hung down nearly to his shoulder.

"We will take care of this—I promise you," Lieutenant Jordan was saying. "These men will be punished, and most severely. They will never do anything like this ever again. You have my word on that."

Although I didn't understand their words, many of the crowd clearly didn't approve of what was taking place. Every time the man in the black suit said something, they raised their fists into the air, shouted loudly, and moved in even closer.

Stretching up on my tiptoes to get a better view, I saw two American servicemen, hands tied behind their backs, leaning awkwardly back against the cargo ramp. Every time the crowd moved, Lieutenant Jordan shifted with them, as if trying to block the view of the trussed Americans.

Lieutenant Jordan indicated he wanted a moment with the rest of his crew. The three of them huddled close and removed wallets from their pockets. Lieutenants Dunning and Dix handed over what cash they had, and soon Lieutenant Jordan turned and faced the man again.

"Here," he said, giving him the money. "I know it will not make up for everything, but I'd like to give it to you as a sign of good faith—a sign that we will take full responsibility for this. These men are not typical Americans. Please don't judge us by their actions. We will take care of this and make this right. Please."

Looking down at the money, the older man smiled before turning and shaking the bills toward the crowd. They didn't cheer, but they did settle down

The older man said to Lieutenant Jordan, "I have your promise?"

"You do. Yes."

Without another word, he motioned for the crowd to follow him down a path toward the city. None spoke as they left.

"What was that all about?" I asked, finally moving toward Lieutenant Jordan. When I came into view, the other Americans, who I now saw were privates and looked absolutely filthy, snapped to attention, quite a feat considering where their hands were.

Chuck said, the disgust clear in his voice, "If it were my decision, we'd have left them here. And what did we get for sticking out necks out? Broke. That's what. Flat broke. Red, you do realize that was every cent we had. Now what are we going to do?"

One of the privates laughed. That is, he did so until Lieutenant Jordan's icy stare shut him up. Turning to me, he said, "We did it because they're Americans. That's the only reason. I was told there was a firing squad waiting for them in the morning, and I couldn't let that happen here. Not to ours—no matter what they've done."

"What did they do?" I asked, moving closer.

The private who laughed cut in and asked, "Hey, you want to untie us now? Sure would be nice."

"No!" Lieutenant Jordan replied, coldly. "Not while that group can still see you. And if I don't get some answers now—and I mean fast—you might stay that way the whole time you're with us. Let's be clear about that. Now, spill it. All of it."

"OK, fair enough," the laugher said. "I'm Private Jim Sims, and this is Private Elroy Jones. We're with the 189th Air Reconnaissance Group just put at Geneina. That is, we were until just over a week ago. Germans got us about ten miles west of here. Elroy and I bailed out, but as soon as we cleared, there was a fireball. Nobody else made it. We walked through that rotten sand two days and nights before we got here. Still can't believe we made it."

Private Jones took over. "They were real nice to us at first. Everybody. Thought we were heroes or something. Put us up in a fancy hotel and fed us till we were full as ticks."

"So, what happened? Why this?" Lieutenant Dix asked, pointing to the ropes around their wrists.

"It all happened so fast," Private Sims jumped back in. "The second night was when all this started. First of all, nobody drinks around here. Against their religion or something. Anyway, a man's got to have something to do to have fun, right? And I don't think the women here would take off that garb for love or money. Leastways, not for money."

Looking over at me, he said, quietly, "Sorry, Ma'am." Then he continued. "So, they don't drink, and they don't chase girls. What else is there?"

"Gambling!" they both shouted in unison. They laughed again, but only for a moment. Jones said. "One of the porters at the hotel told us about a dice game taking place a couple streets over in the back of one of them smokehouses. You know— where they puff away on a hose attached to a big pot. So, anyways, it turns out gambling is illegal, too, and you can really get in trouble for that."

Private Sims kicked him hard on the shin and said, "Don't you think they can see that!" He picked up the tale. "We had a few bucks on us, so we go to the game. Figured it was craps, like in backstreet Cleveland. Boy, were we wrong. They were playing a game called Rinka. It was easy to learn. Based on threes. You know, three, six, nine, twelve. You make your bet, roll two dice, and if any of those threes come up, you win the pot—what everybody has bet against you. If you lose, your money and the money others bet on you gets split up by the rest. And you can make side bets with others around the circle, too. That's where the real money is. It's a fast game, and you can win a lot or lose a lot in a blink of an eye."

"Get to it!" Lieutenant Dix urged again. "What *happened?*"

"Well," Sims continued, "*Genius* here got a brilliant idea."

"It wasn't just my idea!" Private Jones protested. "Yours, too!"

"I'm telling the story," Private Sims cut back in. "Elroy decided it would be easy to load a set of these dice. And it worked, too. They play every night, so the next night we go back and clean up. Lost a little here and there to make it look good, but our pockets were crammed full of cash before daybreak."

"So, what *happened!*" Lieutenant Dix asked again, growing more and more impatient.

Private Sims replied, "I'm gettin' to that. We did this three nights in a row. I kept telling 'em all Americans had this kind of luck, but they were starting to get suspicious. By the end of that third night, we practically owned the place. Four suitcases of those big bills they have here, four camels, and a goat named Baba. Got a house, too. Haven't seen it yet, but I hear it's nice and not far out."

Lieutenant Jordan turned away, shaking his head. Chuck nearly doubled over in laughter. Lieutenant Dix, still not satisfied, said, "One more time. What *happened!*"

Private Sims added, "OK—here's what got us. Apparently, around this place a guy's left hand is considered dirty and evil. Elroy's a left-handed shooter, and he had the loaded pair palmed so that he could do the switch-a-roo as needed. He had just won part interest in a fruit stand when the owner got mad and grabbed at Elroy's hand and pried it open to spit on it. We found out fast what some extra dice will get you. Apparently, it's against the law to gamble but not to admit you've been taken for a ride while doin' it. So, they hog-tied us and took us to jail."

Here he swung his arms around to the side and shook them, as if asking to be untied. Lieutenant Dix shook his head and said, "No! Continue!"

Private Jones spoke up. "We were locked up two days before we got some kind of hearing—right there in the jail. We had a sort of lawyer who told us not to worry, that it'd all be over quickly. Turned out, he meant it wouldn't be long before we were goin' to get shot! And, they'd have done it, too, if you hadn't come along."

"So, who was that young girl who came to get me not long after we landed?" Lieutenant Jordan asked. "The one who told me about you. If it hadn't been for her, this would have been your last night."

Private Sims smiled and said, "Elroy won her, too. Said he was going to start his own harem."

That did it for me. I broke down and laughed until I thought I'd choke. Lieutenant Dix soon followed suit.

Finally, Lieutenant Jordan urged us all to quiet down. "I don't know what to do with you two, but I guess we can't leave you here. But, we probably should."

We started laughing again—until four loud explosions, one right after the other, erupted off in the distance in what looked like the center of El Fasher. After a few moments, Lieutenant Jordan said, quietly, "Looks like the Sudanese have their own problems, too."

The laughter stopped as we stood there and watched the flames shoot high into the air.

$\approx$

Chapter 8

Under Fire

O635 Zulu, January 19
El Fasher, Egyptian Sudan

We could not have asked for better, and more gracious, hosts. The Sudanese had welcomed us in every way with open arms at a time when we badly needed assistance. In a final gesture of kindness, just before we were to leave, they loaded us up with more medical supplies and food for the ship. Their goodwill rejuvenated and fortified us. It was difficult to say our goodbyes, more than any of us could put into words.

After the engines were started and right before we closed the cargo door, Nurse Nazari came running up. "Take this," she said, tossing something up to me. It was a plum, purple-ripe and ready to eat. As I rolled it between my palms, I knew it was more than a piece of fruit. It was connection, a bond, her way of saying we all needed to take care of each other in these trying times. I smiled and waved. Then Sam closed and secured the door.

The takeoff was smooth, and we were soon at cruising altitude. As was now becoming his habit—and I was glad of it— Chuck came down the aisle to visit with us.

He talked about the crew staying aboard the previous night to make sure nothing happened to the plane and the fact they got very little sleep because smaller explosions kept going off in the town every couple of hours. Couldn't have proved it by me. I had decided to sleep in the room with the patients and was out the minute my head hit the pillow.

Chuck also told us, laughing softly off and on as he did, that we now had a couple of extra passengers until they figured out what to do with them. I hadn't noticed them when we were loading the patients. But now looking up, I saw them: Privates Sims and Jones wrapped in blankets behind the cockpit. Both saw me peering their direction and waved. I waved back and tried to give at least a semblance of a smile.

"What do you think you'll do with them?" I asked, shaking my head.

"Really don't know," Chuck replied. "On the one hand, I guess because they didn't try to report to the authorities right away after they chuted, *technically* they could be called deserters. On the other hand, they've been through a lot—losing the rest of their crew and all. Red will figure it out. His decision—not mine. In the meantime, I told them to stay away from you and your patients."

"Oh, I don't think they're too bad," I said. "Just a little mixed up I guess." Pointing over to Corporal Ernst, who was already sleeping again, I added, "People handle stress in different ways. Some sleep it off. Others, well, do sort of what they did. I'm not condoning their actions, but I think I can understand some of it."

Chuck leaned back and said, "Well, we'll see just how understanding you are—and not just about them. I've something else to tell you now. You aren't the only one who has been harboring a secret."

He paused here to call Sam over and make sure none of the others were listening before he continued. "We couldn't tell you before, and I don't want you to worry about this. It won't take us off our schedule very much. But, we're not going straight to Accra today. We're making a detour."

"A detour?" I said, too loudly. "What on earth . . . "

"Shhhh!" he said, putting a finger to my lips. "Let me explain. We're going to shoot southwest to Kano in Nigeria. There's a British supply depot there and a field hospital. We'll refuel there, but we'll also get another passenger at the same time. This one gets the special treatment."

"Is he badly wounded?" Sam jumped in. "Another for us to take home?"

Chuck smirked. "He is wounded, but that's not why we're going to give him a ride. Seems he's a congressman's son, and we've been ordered to get him and take him with us to Accra. We've also been ordered not to let anything else happen to him because it looks like he's going home, for good, from there. His dad must be a pretty important man is all I can say."

"Oh, my!" I said. "He must be in pretty terrible shape if they can't take care of him at the field hospital there. I just hope we can care for him properly until Accra. I know there's one of our station hospitals there."

"Well, first things first," Chuck said, blowing out a breath. "Let's grab him, and we'll see what's what."

Smiling again, he said, "Anything I can do for you this morning, Boom Boom? Thought of you all night because of those booms off in the city."

"No, Books, why don't you get back up there and thumb through a magazine like a good boy."

"Ouch!" he said, stepping back. "Guess I know when I'm not wanted."

"But you are wanted," Sam piped in, laughing.

"Sam!" I said, swatting him hard at the elbow. "And by the way, isn't it your turn to check our patients? Better get going—*both* of you."

As they walked away, Chuck looked back once and waved. I just shook my head and shooed him on.

∾

The landing in Kano took me completely off guard. Once the wheels touched the ground, the force of slowing down pulled us forward so intensely it was difficult to keep everything in place.

I clutched at Private Montague's stretcher and dug my heels into the floor while asking Sam, "Is this what they mean by landing on a postage stamp?"

He laughed, then fell hard against the wall, righting himself quickly to help keep Lieutenant Collin's stretcher from breaking free.

As soon as we stopped, Sam unlatched the cargo door and flung it open. Even though it was well before noon, the air rushing in to greet us was stifling hot. "A furnace," was all Sam said, turning to me. "Don't know how people can live here."

Lieutenant Jordan told us to stay aboard the ship while he and Chuck went to see about the congressman's son. Sam and I used the time to pass around fresh fruit and cups of a very aromatic tea that had been provided by our hosts back at El Fasher. I didn't know how much I was allowed to tell them about our stop, so I just matter-of-factly explained that we had to pick up another injured man and take him along with us. It didn't faze them at all. Private Scalini shrugged and asked, "Got another fig?"

Privates Sims and Jones came back to join us, and for the next thirty minutes regaled us with story after story about their *heroic* acts earlier in the war, all of which I was sure were completely made up. Especially their tale of saving the life of a princess who had been kidnapped by thugs near where their squadron had been stationed in Egypt. However, I didn't mind. The laughter they brought forth was the best medicine the men could have received. I even played along at one point when they said they had found a box of ancient Egyptian jewels one day while digging latrine holes—but the officers took it away from them. When a couple scoffed, I joined in and said, "Why, I think I remember reading about that. You two should have been allowed to keep them. Finders, keepers, you know. That should be the rule." Both looked at me, stunned for a moment, and then Private Sims picked up the story again.

Finally, I saw Chuck walking back toward us. "Lower the ramp," he said, the disappointment clear in his voice as he pointed to the ground. "Looks like we'll be here a while. German air patrols expected somewhere around here over the next few hours, so we've been invited to bring everyone down to their field hospital while we wait it out. Might as well, especially since they said they have some fresh meat they're willing to share with us."

"And what about our new passenger?" I asked. "Where's he? How's he doing?"

"We'll talk about that when you and I walk back." He turned to Sam. "I need to borrow her right now. The Brits are sending up some men to help you. Would appreciate it if you could get everyone down to the hospital and settled in."

"Yo! Not a problem. I'll see to it," Sam replied, saluting smartly.

Chuck saluted him back. "Well, then see to it. We need to be off."

I followed him several yards before he said anything. "You won't believe this," he said. "I don't know what you'd call it in medical terms, but I've got my own description for our new passenger. The word is jerk. Oh, I can think of some stronger ones, but I'm not going to say them in front of you."

"What do you mean?" I asked. "What's wrong?"

"I've never met anybody so arrogant in all my life. The Brits have had it with him. That's probably the real reason we were asked here. They want to get him off their hands."

"Whatever are you talking about? What . . . "

Chuck cut me off, grinning. "Just you wait. You'll see."

The road snaked back and forth around a series of large sand dunes. Once we came to the edge of the last one, the field hospital came into view. "Just look at that!" I said, throwing up my hands. "Wow! It's *huge!*"

I did a quick count. British Field Hospital, Kano, was composed of thirty-four large tents all placed in a circle formation. The largest tent of all, obviously the headquarters and tent number thirty-five, was in the center of the ring, and wide paths extended out from it to the individual tents in the circle.

Chuck reached over, took my hand in his, and urged me on. Realizing what he'd done, so innocently, he jerked away and said, "Sorry! Didn't mean to . . . "

"Not a problem," I said, smiling. "Was feeling a little unsteady in this sand. Glad for the assistance, actually."

"Unsteady? You? I don't believe it, Boom Boom. Not you!"

We both laughed again, entered the circle, and made our way toward the headquarters. As we did, I could see most of the tents closest to us were empty, which I thought odd."

As soon as we were through the tent flaps at headquarters, we were met by Lieutenant Jordan and the base commander, Colonel Ashton Towne, a short, middle-aged man with a bushy, white moustache that curled up at the sides. He wore the British "short pants" uniform, his legs bare from the knees on down. It was so hot, I understood the reason why and was immediately jealous.

"This is Nurse Ott," Lieutenant Jordan said, stepping forward. "Sir, I'd like her to take a look at him, if you don't mind."

Colonel Towne moved toward me, took my hands in his, and said, "A sight for sore eyes. That's what you are. We'll have to send an escort with you at all times here. A pleasure—a true pleasure—to meet you, Lieutenant."

"What he really means," Lieutenant Jordan said, laughing, "is that you're going to be very popular around here."

"You see, all the nurses were evacuated last night when word came that the Germans and Italians might be working up a counter-attack to get some of the real estate back. So, that makes you the only woman for miles around."

"Doesn't seem like a problem to me," I said, laughing with them. "I'm going to look pretty good now. Probably better than I ever have!"

"Right, so," Colonel Towne responded, flicking at his moustache. "Quite!"

"Colonel," Lieutenant Jordan interrupted. "We're on a pretty tight schedule. With your permission, we'd like to take her to see him now."

"Have a go," he said, shaking his head. "He wouldn't let my doctors near him. Cheeky fellow. Rude as a rotten biscuit. Glad you'll take him off our hands."

Colonel Towne motioned to a corporal who had been standing at attention in the corner, a rifle clutched to his chest. The corporal walked over and said, "If you please, this way."

Once we were outside and headed down a path to our left, Lieutenant Jordan said to me, "Glad you're here. Check him out, and we'll haul him out. We've got to leave here—and soon."

We stepped through a double set of flaps at tent number fourteen, and there on an exam table sat our new patient, his legs swinging back and forth. He was flinging playing card off toward a helmet on the ground a few feet away. His aim hadn't been good. I didn't see a one even close to the helmet. The bars on his shirt showed him also to be a lieutenant, but when he looked up and saw us, he didn't stand to salute. Instead, he barked, "About time you got back here." Looking at me, he said, "What's *that?*"

Before the others could say anything, I stepped toward him. "I'm Nurse Ott. I see your arm's bandaged pretty heavily. Let's take a look."

He recoiled, jerking his arm completely behind his back so I couldn't touch it. "And just who do you think you are?" he said, snarling. "You're not a doctor. I said I wanted an American doctor. Not some . . . some . . . traveling nurse."

Turning away from me and flinging the cards again toward the helmet, he added, "You're not going to touch me. Understand!"

"That'll be enough of that, Mister!" Chuck said, rushing toward him. Lieutenant Jordan grabbed Chuck's shoulder and pulled him back.

"You don't talk to my people that way," Lieutenant Jordan barked at him. "I don't care who you are. Right now, you're nothing but a wounded body. That's all. And, if you don't let her check you over, guess what? You don't get to leave here. Those are the rules. So what do you want? She checks you—or you stay here and rot. I think I'll leave this up to you."

Lieutenant Jordan walked around the table so that he was right in front of him. "One more thing—and let's get this understood. See these bars on my shoulder. I'm a grade higher than you, so I'm your superior officer. Ever heard of insubordination? I can slap you with that so fast your head would spin off. Got that?"

He looked up and said, in a slow, condescending voice, "Nobody'd believe you. Would be your word against mine. And who do you think they'd believe?"

Both Lieutenant Jordan and Chuck looked ready to explode when he quickly added, "But I want out of this hole. She can look at my arm, but I don't want anyone else in here. Understood?"

I knew I needed to step in to keep the pot from boiling completely over, so I said, "That can be done." Pointing to the others, I said, "Go ahead. It'll be fine. I'll call if I need anything. Please step outside."

The corporal pointed to a metal cabinet off in the corner and said, "Ma'am, medical supplies are there. Help yourself."

They all started to leave, but Chuck turned one last time and said, but not for my benefit, "I'll be *just* outside."

Once they had gone, I walked over and took his wrist to take his pulse. He tried pulling away, but I held firm and started counting aloud. "What's your name, Soldier?" I asked, letting go of his wrist and checking his forehead for signs of fever.

"I'm just a *wounded body,*" he said, screwing up his face and mocking Lieutenant Jordan's description.

"Got to have a name, don't you?" I asked, moving closer to check pupil reaction to light. "Most everyone has one. Mine's Ott, but everyone calls me Boom Boom."

I thought that might get at least a small smile, but instead he mocked *me* this time, "Boom Boom? Why that? Are you gassy? Eat a lot of beans, do you?"

"Now that's funny," I deadpanned, roughly pulling his left ear toward me so I could look inside. "Not bad at all."

"Ouch!" he protested, slapping my hand away. "What's with you, *Boom Boom?*"

"Let's look at that arm now," I said, reaching for it. He again swung it behind his back. "Remember what they said. If I don't check it, you stay here. What will it be?"

"Just don't yank on it like you did my ear. You don't have a good touch at all."

"I'll be gentle," I said as he slowly extended his left arm toward me. "I promise."

The bandaging was so excessive it took more than a minute to unwrap it. When the last of it rolled off, I looked for a dressing of some sort over a wound—but I saw neither. No dressing. No wound.

"Who did the bandages?" I asked, still looking up and down his arm.

"I did," he replied, glaring at me. "Couldn't find a doctor when I got hurt. Did a great job, didn't I?"

"That depends," I said, gently squeezing up and down his arm, trying to find some sort of injury. "What happened to you? How were you hurt?"

Here he mumbled and stammered a few moments before blurting out, "I guess I'm better now. Couldn't move it for a week. Black and blue all over. Probably a bone cracked in there somewhere. Felt like it, so I wrapped it. What else could I do?"

"I see," I said, folding my arms and stepping back. "Well, it appears to be much improving." I bit my lip a little to keep from laughing. "Glad of that. Do you think we should re-wrap it—or give it some air?"

His eyes widened as he said, seriously, "Oh, wrap it. Still needs it. I can tell." He raised his shoulder a little and winced, looking over to make sure I saw it.

"One thing I can sure do is wrap. Here we go."

I used nearly a whole roll of wide cotton bandage, from wrist to shoulder. So much, in fact, by the time I was finished he could barely bend his arm. But, he didn't complain. There's an old expression: "You don't tease a snake with a stick." Well, I think he looked at me at that point as his snake, one that could bite him pretty good if I wanted to after seeing the extent of the damage to his arm.

"There you go," I said, using adhesive gauze to hold everything in place at both ends. "That'll do it. I believe you're ready for travel. I'll go tell the others."

I half expected him to thank me, at least to some small degree, but all he did was look at me and smirk. I didn't want to give him the satisfaction of seeing me respond to that, so I simply left the tent.

Lieutenant Jordan and Chuck were waiting for me. "Well?" both said at once. "How is he?"

"Before I answer that," I said, motioning them to follow me away from the tent, "I have a couple of questions. What can you tell me about all this? When and where do they say he got hurt?"

Lieutenant Jordon said, "Honestly, I think the truth is he went over the hill about a week ago. He was stationed here with a small American support squad for a few days before he just up and disappeared. The Colonel told me they sent out search parties two days in a row and didn't find a single trace of him. Probably was in Kano somewhere—sharing his charming disposition with those poor people. I'd guess they probably threw him out. He finally came back here with that arm bandaged. Said he'd been kidnapped by locals while taking a walk outside the compound and was being held for ransom when he broke free. Said he wrecked up his arm during the escape. Made such a fuss about it that Colonel Towne called the American Command down in Accra and relayed the story—and said they didn't know what to do because he refused to let any of the doctors here examine him. Our boys checked into his record, found out who his pappy is, and because they were also told he was wounded, well, here we are."

"Yeah, here we are," Chuck said, his voice solid with disgust. "So, can he travel? What's your diagnosis?"

Before I could answer, Sam walked up and told us all our patients had been taken to the large tent directly across from us. They were being well taken care of and getting fed. We had also been invited to the mess tent for some of the fresh meat we'd heard about earlier, something worth its weight in gold in this region.

"I don't care if it's camel steaks," Sam said, rubbing his stomach. "I'm starved. I need some meat."

"Go ahead," I said. "We'll join you in a few minutes. We'll catch up."

As soon as he had walked several steps away, I turned back to Lieutenant Jordan and Chuck. "What you've said confirms my thoughts. This man is a faker. Nothing wrong with him at all, other than the fact that after I worked on him, he really can't move that arm now. Wrapped him like a mummy, which I guess fits considering where we are. He's just a plain, garden-variety faker, and not a very clever one at that."

"I knew it!" Lieutenant Jordan said, slapping his leg loudly. "We should just take him out behind one of those sand dunes and shoot him. We'd probably get a medal from these people if we did."

"Nothing I'd like better," Chuck added. "But, not our job to deal with all this. We're supposed to get him out of here and drop him off in Accra. I feel sorry for the boys down there. That'll be their problem, though. Let's get rid of him—and the sooner the better."

I had just agreed when suddenly a burst of shots rang out followed by one of the British soldiers screaming, "Take cover! Take cover! Snipers!"

"Get over here!" Lieutenant Jordan called out, waving us to follow him. "Behind these sandbags! Get down and duck!"

Colonel Towne rushed out of headquarters, scanned the compound, and commanded, "To your positions. Rifles up— hold your fire—until you've a clear target. Steady now, men."

The shots continued ringing out, but none of the British fired back. Instead, in movements that had clearly been practiced many times, soldiers with rifles dove behind large piles of sand- bags built up in front of each tent and took up firing positions.

I looked over to the tent where our patients had been taken and saw Sam's head stick out briefly, as if evaluating the situa- tion. "Stay safe," I said to myself. "All of you."

"Everyone OK?" Chuck asked while peering over the highest bag in front of us. Just as he did so, another round of fire erupted. Bullets hit several of the bags around us sending out bursts of sand with each strike.

"Get down!" I yelled, grabbing his leg.

There was still no return fire from the British, so I said, to no one in particular, "Why is everyone just sitting there? Shouldn't we at least try to do *something?*"

"We are doing something," Lieutenant Jordan replied. "We're staying alive."

A few moments later, Chuck leaned over toward him and said, "My sidearm is in the ship. Should have brought it with me. Dumb. Will next time."

"Mine, too," Lieutenant Jordan said, "but a pistol wouldn't do much good at this distance. We'll just have to ride this out."

We stayed huddled close together the better part of an hour. All we could do was keep a sharp lookout. We didn't talk at all, which made the time crawl. Occasionally, I peered around one of the bags to watch the waves of heat rising from the tops of the dunes just outside the compound. In minutes, all our clothing was soaked clear through, and every time we shifted, more sand stuck to us, making us even more uncomfortable.

There were long periods of prolonged fire followed by lulls of about equal length. The balance was such that we couldn't tell if it was safe to get up. As I looked around the compound, it was clear everyone else was thinking the same thing—and kept safely behind their bags. I couldn't tell where the bullets were landing. At one point, I thought some had whizzed just over our heads, but I couldn't be sure. So, I kept my head down and prayed.

When one of the lulls grew to over ten minutes, Colonel Towne ordered the soldiers crouched behind bags at the forward tents to scout out the situation. A few minutes later, they came back and ran over to him. Soon, Colonel Towne called out, "Men, all clear! Check for damage. Let's be up and about!"

When I felt it was safe enough, I walked over to him. "Colonel, I'd like to help with the wounded. Just let me know where to report."

"Won't be any," he said, glancing around at the men emerging from behind the sandbags.

"But all those bullets—they were everywhere," I said, pointing around the compound.

Shielding his eyes from the sun and still looking off in the distance, he replied, "So far, they don't try to kill us. They want us pinned down so they can rob us blind. Happens all the time. If they killed us and we weren't here, that would be the end of the Golden Goose, wouldn't it? They're smart enough to know that. They've taken tents, food supplies, weapons—and a bloody truck last week. Lousy, dirty. . ."

"I'm sorry, Colonel. That's terrible."

"Yes, it is. But we'll catch up to them eventually. You mark my words." He called over a sergeant, and they started walking back toward headquarters.

I walked back over to Chuck and Lieutenant Jordan, who still didn't seem much interested in leaving the safety of the sandbags. "I'm sure glad that's over!" I said, brushing sand from my sleeves and skirt. "I better go check on the patients and Sam now."

"And we'll check the ship," Chuck said. As he turned to leave, he said, "You didn't seem too scared during all that. You're really something, Boom Boom."

"Don't you kid yourself," I said, my voice sharp. "I was scared all the way down to my G.I. shoes. Didn't have time to show it though. Like Paul said, I was just trying to stay alive."

It was the first time I had called Lieutenant Jordan by his first name. After what we'd just been through together, it seemed to me all of that military formality could be pitched out the window. Or, in this case, behind one of the nearby sand dunes. He didn't scold me, and the look on his face made me believe he felt the same. He smiled and said, softly, "You take care of yourself until we get back. Don't forget—we're still responsible for you." With that, they both headed back to the plane.

I walked over to see our patients. All were fine, except for rattled nerves. Lieutenant Collins gripped his stretcher for emphasis and said, "I felt like a sitting duck. I hate this. Nothing I could do but lie here. If I had my Lightning I'd sure show these snipers a thing or two."

"And I believe you would," I said, taking his hand. "Don't you worry. You'll be back in this fight real soon."

I said it, but I knew it wasn't true. He was staring at a very delicate spine operation back home that had potential to turn either way. Still, I wanted to offer him some hope. I wanted him to feel he'd soon be useful again. What he most needed was his dignity.

The others greeted me quietly as I checked over each of them. Captain Goldman's tuberculosis fever had spiked again, so I asked one of the orderlies to administer a good dose of aspirin. Private Montague didn't complain about his bedsores, but I could tell by the way he was rocking back and forth on the stretcher that he needed attention—and the sooner the better. When I got to Private Scalini, I saw he was seated in front of

Corporal Ernst, holding his hand. He looked up and said, "The shots really spooked him. When they first went off, he grabbed me and still hasn't let go. I don't mind, though."

Private Scalini might not have had much vision left, but he saw more than most would have in this situation. As I passed, I patted Private Scalini gently on the shoulder and said, "Thanks."

Sam and I had just finished updating the charts when Chuck stormed into the tent. He took a few seconds to catch his breath, then said, "We've been robbed! All your medical supplies. And the ship's tires slashed."

My mouth dropped open as he continued, "Guards at the strip didn't see a thing."

He blew out a few quick breaths and steadied himself against a tent pole. "Have you seen Private Sims and Jones? Can't find 'em. If you haven't seen 'em, maybe they were captured—or hiding—or run off. Don't know . . . They're gone. And the tires . . . "

Seeing Chuck so full of emotion pushed me to my edge. I could feel tears starting to well up as I asked, "What do we do now? What can we do?"

"I don't know," he said, punching the tent pole, hard, and looking down at the ground. "I honestly don't."

After pausing only a second, he looked up and said, "We're trapped!"

∾

Chapter 9

Pirates

1917 ZULU, January 19
British Field Hospital, Kano, Nigeria

THE REST OF THE AFTERNOON and early evening passed by quickly, especially because we were all so anxious about how and when we'd be able to be on our way again. While Chuck and the rest of the crew scrambled to find a solution, I decided the best thing I could do was keep busy. Once I made sure our men were settled in, I decided to make the rounds of the recovery tents spread around the compound. I wanted to see if I could help, but I had another motivation that I wasn't ashamed to admit. I needed the attention—if nothing else something to distract me from what the snipers had done. I knew I looked a mess, but I also thought I might be able to bring some cheer to the men, especially because I was the only woman in camp.

The greeting each time was just as I expected—cheers and some whistles. I gave it right back to them, complimenting each man on some feature of his face or general physique. The smiles and laughs that came back in return were good for us all.

I was also welcomed warmly by the doctors and orderlies I ran across, so while they tended to duties they had put off earlier in the afternoon when the ruckus had started, I changed a few bandages and sat with some patients. I was just rewrapping a foot when Sam caught up with me and suggested we get a bite to eat. I didn't know when we'd next get a chance for something other than sandwiches, so I agreed to go with him.

The mess tent was in full swing when we arrived, which, I have to admit, really shocked me. Extra security was everywhere—armed soldiers standing both just inside and outside the tent flaps and even at the end of the chow line. However, that wasn't what gave me pause. What did was the fact one would never have known that a few hours before these same men were pinned down and under fire. Laughter and light-hearted banter filled the tent as Sam and I entered.

We picked up our trays and were served ample portions of lima beans and boiled potatoes. Near the end of the line, we were met by a server who asked us, "Fresh meat?"

"Yes, please!" we both said in unison as our excitement grew. However, that excitement didn't last long. It turned out that "fresh meat" we had heard so much about was Spam! The whole group must have been in on the joke because the second the slices hit our trays, laughter and applause filled the air. A corporal in line behind us whispered to me, "We do this to all who visit us. Jolly good fun, right?" I smiled weakly, turned around, and shouted so all could hear me, "I do love your British humor!" Another rousing round of applause followed.

One would have thought we hadn't eaten in weeks. I wasn't overly fond of lima beans, but I didn't miss a one. Even the Spam tasted good. Sam suggested in this part of the world it was made mostly with camel meat. I didn't believe him. It wasn't stringy enough.

"You look bushed," I said to Sam, who had one elbow propping him up as he used his other hand to shovel food to his mouth.

"I could use a few winks," he said, straightening up some. "But, there's still a lot to do. Soon as we're finished here, I better get back to the ship to see if I can help scrounge for new tires, but so far there don't seem to be any available. I don't have to tell you how bad this is. If we have any hope of keeping on schedule . . ."

"I know," I said. "Somehow, I just have to believe it'll all work out."

"I hope you're right," he replied, yawning loudly.

My thoughts about what might happen if I was wrong were interrupted when a young Captain came over and introduced himself. "I'm Hodges," he said. "Mind if I join in for a minute or two?"

He was tall, quite thin, and had one of the British uniform hats with one side rolled up tucked under his left arm.

"Not at all," I replied scooting over on the bench so there was room for him to sit comfortably.

"Terribly sorry about this afternoon," he said, shaking his head. "Not a good way to introduce you to our little hospital here. However, it's happening more these days, and we've no solution yet. We just have to go with it for the time being. So sorry about that. Are all of your party unscathed?"

I assured him we were fine. "Captain, thank you for this wonderful hospitality. All of you have been so good to me—to us—and I extend my deepest thanks for that."

He nodded as I continued. "Sir, if you don't mind, nobody has told us who was shooting at us. It couldn't have been the Germans, right? Aren't they all farther north now?"

"Bloody renegades," he said, his voice tightening. "Locals, all of them. Bands of them everywhere. They stole from the Italians when they were here. Then from the Jerrys. Now us. They fight for themselves and don't care a whit for what we're all fighting for. They've been at war with somebody for centuries. In their blood, I would suppose."

"But don't they know their lives would be better with us, the Allies, than with Hitler? They have to know that, don't they?"

"I've decided their freedom is their fighting. That is to say, it's all they seem to know. They remind me of wasps that want nothing more than to sting. Can't exterminate the lot, though, so we fight them off when we can and live with what they steal and ruin. Nothing else we can do. God knows we've tried."

He glanced at his watch. "Just wanted to welcome you and let you know you can come to me should you require anything during your stay, which I hope will be a long one."

He stood, bowed slightly toward me, clicked the heels of his shoes together, and was off.

"I like the British," I said to Sam. "Polished and polite. Good manners. Not bad looking, either."

"Better not let Lieutenant Dunning hear you say that," he teased, offering me a spoonful of lima beans. "He'd most likely have a fit, you know."

I just glared at him and squinted my eyes. He put his lima beans back on his tray and said, "OK—just thought I'd better mention it."

We ate in silence a few minutes, but Sam looked up and said he had one more thing he felt I should know before he went off to liberate a few medical supplies.

"When I went back to the ship right after the attack, I saw Lieutenant Dix sitting by one of the cut tires. He was cursing a blue streak and pounding his fist on the ground."

"So? He was mad. So am I. We all are."

"Yeah, he's mad, but I found out from your boyfriend the reason it hit him the hardest. That Able Mable on the nose. That's a painting of his fiancée. I mean, she was his fiancée. She was killed in one of the blitz bombings in London. The ship was dedicated to her, and whenever something happens to it, well, he takes it like he did today. Thought you should know."

"Thanks for telling me," I said, putting down my fork.

I couldn't eat another bite, but it wasn't because I was full.

≈

"Wake up! Wake up!" Chuck quietly urged me while shaking my shoulders. "We've got to move. Now!"

"What time is it?" I asked. "It's still pitch black . . ."

"No time to explain. Please, just get up. We'll talk on the ship."

I looked over and saw Sam already leading Private Scalini toward the tent opening. Turning to me, he whispered, "Be back in a minute. Get Captain Goldman ready. I've got help coming for the stretchers. Got to get everyone on board as fast as we can. Hop to it!"

I was still yawning and rubbing sleep from my eyes when Privates Sims and Jones ran inside the tent. "Sorry, Ma'am," Sims said, stopping only long enough to half way salute. Jones did the same. "Which one you want us to take first?" Sims asked, pointing to both Lieutenant Collins and Private Montague.

"Him," I replied, indicating Private Montague. "Be easy as you can. His back's been hurting pretty bad."

I had been napping on a cot just in front of the men, so I was in the way. I shoved my cot back against the tent wall, and got busy, still not knowing why I was doing it. Another sniper attack? I couldn't hear any gunfire. Morning come earlier than I thought? No—a quick glance at my watch showed four in the morning. My mind still foggy with sleep, I decided all I could do was trust Chuck and follow his orders.

Captain Goldman and Corporal Ernst were already awake, so I urged both up, took each by the hand, and said, "You heard 'em. Let's get out of here." Captain Goldman asked why we were in such a hurry, but all I could do was be honest with him and say I didn't have the slightest clue. Corporal Ernst, as typical, didn't utter a sound as he followed along.

It took less than five minutes for all of us to be aboard. I could see the crew checking instruments and charts—with Private Sims standing close behind them. He appeared to be talking up a storm as he pointed through the cockpit windows. As soon as I sat down, the engines roared to life. Sam pulled the cargo door shut, and not even a minute later, we were off down the runway and lifting into the air.

We hadn't even leveled off when Sam unbuckled and got up to make sure the men were all doing well. When he finally sat down again, I couldn't stand it any longer.

"Somebody better tell me," I said to him, sharply. "What in the world just happened?"

He smiled. "We're pirates now. Sneaking off before we get a good British flogging."

"What are you talking about? Make some sense."

"I'm so proud of 'em I could hug 'em both."

"Who?"

"Sims and Jones. While we were sleeping, you know what those two knotheads did? They got us tires. Got them right off one of the Brits' cargo planes. Not exactly the same size, but Lieutenant Jordan said they'd do just fine until we get replacements."

"Didn't anyone see them?" I asked, stunned by the revelation.

"That's the best part. Got the Brit ground crew to help them do it! Seems there was some sort of dice game involved—and blackmail. The Brits get terrible punishment if they're caught gambling on base. I mean bad punishment. From what I heard, not only did Sims and Jones pick them clean with the dice, they said they'd spill the beans about the game if some tires weren't found right away."

Sam laughed heartily. "Know what they did next? They said they'd give back all the money if the crew would help—and promised to keep quiet. Just told them to blame the tires on the snipers. Guess the ground crew must have thought it best to get us out of here fast to be on the safe side, so here we are. That's why we were in such a hurry. Had to get away before they found out about their cargo plane being stripped—and before questions started."

He paused to catch his breath and said, laughing even louder, "And Sims and Jones somehow ended up away with their money, too!"

I simply couldn't believe it. "You're joking, aren't you? How could they . . . "

At that point, I looked around and realized we were also once again fully stocked with medical supplies, everything from bandages to new bottles of aspirin tablets—even two crates of

British canned rations. "And they got all this, too?" I asked waving my arm around.

"Well, they didn't get *everything,*" he replied, smiling broadly.

"Brother, you weren't kidding when you said we're pirates." Pointing to him, I added, "Looks like we all are."

I looked toward the cockpit and saw Sims and Jones sitting down, settling against the wall, and covering themselves up with blankets. I was just about to go up and thank them before they drifted off to sleep when Chuck started walking back, tapping them both on their helmets as he passed.

"Did you hear?" Chuck asked, smiling. "Understand now?"

"Really think we can get away with this?" I asked.

"We already did," was his reply. "Clean as a whistle, too."

It was then something else came to me in a flash. I stood, looked around, and said, "Wait a minute. We're missing one. Where's the congressman's son? What happened to him?"

"Guess he's back at Kano. That's a shame, isn't it?"

Sam burst out in laughter—and I joined in. "By the way," I finally said, "I never even found out his name. Who is he?"

"Who?" Chuck asked, suddenly becoming serious. "Why, I don't have any idea who you're talking about?"

We all laughed again as Chuck headed back toward the cockpit.

≈

Chapter 10

Farewell, *Able Mabel*

0745 ZULU, January 20
Accra, British Gold Coast

I knew we were incredibly lucky to be back on schedule, but a wave of sadness washed over me as soon as our wheels touched down at Accra. This was as far as we'd be going with *Able Mabel*, which meant Chuck would soon be off on other duty. I had known him only a few days, but long enough my heart hurt at the thought. The past few years I had been so busy with my nurse training and the war—and had been moved around so much—I had little opportunity to form any deep friendships, especially with men. Chuck was the first in a long time to make me laugh, to make me feel good all over. And now he would soon be gone. Sam noticed me staring out the window and said, as if he knew exactly what I was thinking, "It doesn't have to be the end. Trust me."

Lieutenant Dix had radioed ahead, so a full complement of orderlies was waiting for us when we taxied to the main gate by the conning tower. At long last, we were finally at an air base under American control with an American hospital, the 167th Station Hospital. The Sudanese and Brits had been wonderful to us, but it was a great feeling being surrounded by our own countrymen once again.

Because we had so much help, Sam and I talked it over and decided he would go to the hospital with our patients while I visited the Base Commander to get everything lined up for the next leg of the journey. That division of labor seemed to make sense, so we went our separate ways.

I asked a jeep driver if he could give me a lift to Headquarters, and he was happy to do so. Headquarters here was a large, rectangular, one-story structure with small windows spaced evenly along its whole length—all with thick bars across them. The building looked more like a prison than a military establishment. Once inside, I announced myself to a corporal who said, "Lieutenant, we've been expecting you. Please sit over there. I'll let the Colonel know you're here. He'll be with you shortly."

I had just flipped a few pages through an old *Life* magazine when the office door opened, and the Colonel motioned me in. He was not at all what I expected. Most senior officers I had known were all "spit and polish," traditional down to the laces of their shoes. The young man before me was anything but that. He did have on a regular-issue Army shirt, but it was unbuttoned a good four inches down from the top, revealing a shock of his thick chest hair. His sleeves were also rolled up past his elbows, and I noticed a large, brown, irregularly-shaped stain at the button just above his belt. Most dressed in such a state would face a fairly severe reprimand. However, he was at the top and free to do as he wished. I did wonder, however, if others around the base appeared the same. If they were, this base was run by a group of ragamuffins.

"Lieutenant Ott, please come in. I'm Colonel Whiting. This way."

Once we were both seated, he leaned back and said, "You must be something pretty special. Got a personal call from General Grant, the Air Surgeon himself. He instructed me to give any and all aid to you—and not to ask too many questions either. Now, I'm a curious man by nature, so I'm still wondering what's going on here."

He paused and looked intently at me, as if hoping I would provide at least a crumb of information.

"I sincerely wish I could fill you in," I said. "But, the fact of the matter is I'm also very much in the dark about all of this myself. I was given strict orders to get these men back to Walter Reed as quickly as I could. I'm honestly not sure of the reasons why, but I do know somebody feels this mission is very important.

"It isn't me, Sir. I'm not important. I'm an average nurse trying to do her job. Just at the right place at the right time, I suppose. That's all I can guess. All I know for sure right now is I was supposed to report to you and get a new ship to take us the rest of the way home."

"Hmmmmm," he said, picking up a pencil and tapping it on his desk. "Not going to talk, are you? I like that. Always best to keep a mouth shut in situations like this. Looks like they picked the right woman for the job. Most women can't keep a secret, but it appears you can."

I was offended—and wanted to tell him most men I knew were bigger blabbermouths than any woman I could think of, but I let it go. All I wanted at that moment was the new ship.

Before I could question the Colonel about our new ship, the corporal rapped several times at the door and stuck his head in. "They're here, Sir. Should I send 'em in?"

The Colonel nodded, and in a few moments two lieutenants walked in, saluting him smartly.

"Gentlemen, this is Lieutenant Elsie Ott. Lieutenant Ott, this is Lieutenant Tom Forbes and Lieutenant Jack Tucker. They'll be your escorts from here on."

They were so much alike they looked as if they could have been twins. Same height, same build, same baby-face features, same blonde, wavy hair—even the same shine gloss on their black shoes. The only difference I could tell at all was Forbes had blue eyes, and Tucker's were green. I guessed them to be in their early twenties at best, although I knew they had to have had some significant flying experience to get this far along.

"Pleased to meet you," both said, shaking my hand. Once both were seated, Lieutenant Forbes offered some reassuring words. "We'll get you there. I promise you that. We've been told you're to have whatever you want. Guess you must be pretty special."

Colonel Whiting burst out laughing. "Same thing I said just a moment ago, boys. But, she's tight-lipped. Don't think you'll get too much out of her. So, do what she says and move her down the line. Maybe we'll all be told something later."

Looking at his watch, he said, "Give her the lowdown on your ship, but make it snappy."

"I'm your co-pilot," Lieutenant Tucker began. "We'll give you and the wounded as smooth a ride as we can. Our ship is a B-24 Liberator that's been re-done for special duty. We've hauled troops and supplies everywhere from South America to China. For this mission, we've had mattresses put in the bomb bay section because we've no way to anchor stretchers anywhere. It's not tough to get down there, so I don't think you'll find that a problem. One of the advantages of the B-24 is we have plenty of room, so you'll also be able to get about and stretch your legs when you need to. Our ship's a good one. I think it'll do fine for what you need."

He paused and looked at both Colonel Whiting and Lieutenant Forbes before continuing. "There is one thing, though, that came up just this morning. Seems we're going to have some extra passengers. Eleven Seabees, to be exact. Colonel, you want to explain this?"

"Yep, eleven dirt movers. They're needed at your first stop, Ascension Island. Ascension is a very valuable piece of real estate right now. It's our only major refueling stop between here and South America. The Germans know it, and they've been doing a pretty darn good job of tearing up that airfield every chance they get. Got 'em really good the other day and killed almost the entire field maintenance crew when a bomb hit their tent. You're taking the replacements. Sorry, but this has to be done, and I've got no other ships available today. That means you're it."

I had been quiet to this point but now jumped in. "Not a problem, Sir. However, I may just put those Seabees to work watching over my patients. Can always use extra hands."

Colonel Whiting smiled. "Somehow, I believe you would." Addressing all of us, he added, pointing to me, "I imagine you need to transfer some supplies to their ship and get yourself organized. Don't let me keep you. You all get together and get your schedule straightened. You're supposed to leave tomorrow at first light. My clerk will see to your clearance. Any questions?"

When we didn't respond, he said, "Good luck, gentlemen—and lady. Let me know if I can do anything else before you go."

Once outside the building, Lieutenant Forbes's first words were, "Did you see how he was dressed? Jeepers!"

Lieutenant Tucker and I both laughed. "Must be the heat," I said, kicking at the dirt. "Maybe he's overcome."

"Maybe," Lieutenant Forbes said. "But someone somewhere up the line is going to nail him one of these days. In the meantime, though, let's get him out of our heads. Guess we've got work to do. Lieutenant Ott, what kind of supplies do you have to move, and what can we do to help?"

We spent the next several minutes sharing information and making our plans as they escorted me toward the hospital. The airfield at Accra was our most important Allied jumping-off point in the whole region, so soldiers were everywhere, giving us plenty to draw from for the tasks we needed done. I had to get our supplies moved, and they were still trying to figure out the best way to anchor inside the ship the tools and equipment they were told the Seabees would be bringing with them. The more we talked, the more it sounded like we'd all be crammed in there like sardines.

"Don't you worry," Lieutenant Tucker reassured me. "We'll get off the ground—somehow. And then let's hope we can stay up." He smiled and used his hand to make the image of a plane crashing down.

"You don't scare me," I said, holding my head high. "I've already done that!"

∽

I was right at the entrance to the hospital when I heard my name called out. I turned, and saw Chuck running toward me. Catching his breath, he said, "Glad I caught you. What's your schedule? What'd you find out?"

"Got another plane. We're all set. Leaving in the morning. At least that's the plan. What about you?"

"I'm not leaving until tomorrow, either. So, that means we'll likely have some free time later on. I'd like to ask you something, Elsie. If your schedule permits, would you do me the honor of allowing me to escort you to a great little restaurant just down the road a piece? I've been there a few times before, and I think you'd enjoy it. And, I'd enjoy your company."

"Why, Lieutenant, I think that would be nice—schedule permitting of course. Why don't we check with each other about, say, eighteen hundred?"

"I'll be right here at the entrance on the dot."

He started to lean forward to hug me but caught himself. Backing up slightly, he said, "I look forward to it."

As soon as he had gone, I entered the hospital and inquired at the reception desk where the men had been taken. The clerk there pointed down the hallway and said, "Room 27—that way."

Sam was still attending to the men when I entered. "How they doing?" I asked, stepping forward to help him rebandage Private Montague's bedsores.

"All things considered, I'd say pretty well. We do, however, need to keep an eye on Captain Goldman. That fever really bothers me. It's still climbing."

Captain Goldman had appeared to be asleep, so he startled us when he opened his eyes and said, his voice muffled through his mask, "Soldier, I'm sick—not deaf. Fever isn't bad as long as it isn't over hundred and three. What is it now?"

"Hundred and two," Sam replied.

Even through the mask we could see he was smiling as he said, "Good. I guess I'll live a day or two longer. Give me some more aspirin, cover me up, and get to those who need the help. I'm not going anywhere."

I walked over and said, "Good diagnosis, Doctor. Yes, I think you'll make it."

All the others, except for Corporal Ernst, were trying to take naps. Corporal Ernst had moved a chair over to the window and was staring outside. I asked if he needed anything, but he didn't respond, didn't move. I squeezed his shoulder and stepped back.

Right then a young nurse walked in and handed a pitcher of water to Sam. She turned to leave, but I practically shouted, "Wait a minute! Don't go!"

I took her by the arm and ushered her into the hallway, closing the door behind us. "Am I glad to see you!" I said as she looked at me curiously. "Look at me. I haven't had a decent shower or clean clothes in days. And look at this hair. I look like a haystack. I need a place to clean up. Can you help me?"

She laughed and said, "Come on. Follow me. We have a nurses' lounge on the other side of the hospital. We'll have you back in order in no time."

I stuck my head back inside the door and told Sam I needed to be away for a while. Turning again to the nurse, I said, while pushing her ahead of me, "Let's go! I've got a date tonight, and I don't want to scare him off when he sees me."

"Got it," she said, quickening her pace. "We'll take care of you."

I actually got a real shower while two other nurses did a "wet sponge" laundering of my uniform, followed by a quick ironing. They even cleaned and polished my shoes. As I was toweling my hair, one of them said to me, "Are they worth it? Do men know what we go through for them?"

"This one might be worth it," I replied. "Don't know for sure yet, but I'm working on it."

We all laughed.

When I felt human again, I went back to the room to relieve Sam and try to catch a nap myself. There were several cots stacked along the back wall, so I pulled one down, opened it, and crawled in. I hadn't realized how tired I was. In just a few moments, I was out.

When I finally woke up and looked at my watch, I was shocked. I had slept two hours. Not only that, I realized I had exactly ten minutes to get to the entrance to meet Chuck. Sam was back and napping in a chair by the door, so I gently shook his shoulder and told him I was leaving and would be back later in the evening. He nodded and closed his eyes again.

Chuck was standing just to the side of the entrance when I rushed out. I hoped to be greeted by a nice smile or a few kind words, but he looked like he had swallowed a lemon as he shook his head side to side.

"What is it? What's wrong?" I asked, moving quickly toward him.

Before he could respond, all became crystal-clear. Stepping out of the bushes where they had been smoking, Sims and Jones shouted, "Hi there, Lieutenant!"

Chuck pointed to them and finally spoke. "Guess who's joining our dinner party tonight?"

"You're kidding," I responded as both snapped to attention and saluted me.

"Wish I was," Chuck said, shaking his head again. "But I'm—we're—stuck with 'em."

"Why? How?" was all I could get out before Chuck inter-rupted me. "Apparently, they're heroes now. When Paul and I had our debriefing with Colonel Whiting, Paul told him about how they liberated the tires from the British and saved our bacon. Paul tried to pin everything on them so we wouldn't be in trouble. Felt they owed us at least that much for not turning them in as deserters. Turns out the Colonel absolutely hates the British, so he's going to put these two up for citations of merit. And get this. Because their unit got moved too far away, they're being sent back to the States for reassignment—and given two weeks of R & R. Do you believe it?"

"But why are they here—with you?"

"Because the Colonel suggested they be rewarded with a night on the town for their bravery and initiative, and he practi-cally ordered me to show them around since I've been to Accra many times before. I'm their guide tonight. Lucky me."

"This is going to be fun," Sims said, rubbing his hands together. "Let's get going."

"What do you think?" Chuck asked, moving toward me. "Looks like if we go, they go. Don't see any way out of this. Tell me you're still game?"

"We won't get in your way," Jones chuckled. "Don't you worry 'bout us. You'll hardly know we're there."

I shook my head several times. Laughing, because it was the only thing I could think to do, I said, "Well, I'd like to be with you tonight, so if this is what it's going to take, at least it should be interesting."

"That's what I'm afraid of," Chuck said, glaring at them. "Ok, you two, fall in and stay behind us. Keep your mouths shut and your hands to yourself—and not in the pockets of anyone going by. Got that?"

"Yes, Sir!" both responded, laughing. "We get it."

Chuck rolled his eyes, took my hand, pointed ahead, and said, loudly, "Forward, ho!"

With that, off we went.

≈

Chapter 11

A Big Gamble

1635 ZULU, January 20
Accra, British Gold Coast

IT WAS A SHORT TAXI RIDE to the Azmera Café, which was more than fine with me. Because of a crate of live chickens on the front seat next to our driver, all four of us had to crowd into the back. I didn't mind Chuck pressed against me, but Sims and Jones never shut up the whole way there. One would point out the window at a shop or a restaurant we were passing, and the other would have to make detailed commentary. Even with Chuck hushing them up repeatedly, they never slowed down.

Finally, Chuck just threw up his hands—no small feat given how cramped we were—and scooted himself enough around we could visit at least some to ourselves. While we made our way along, he shared with me how the Azmera Café had been built specifically to cater to the Americans at the base and all other allied troops who came through the area. This meant, he explained, the food wouldn't be as spicy as was typical for most other restaurants in Accra. The specialty was seafood, caught and prepared within hours of being hauled out of the Atlantic. It sounded wonderful to me—until I looked over at Sims and Jones.

We were given a table toward the back, the perfect romantic spot if not for our tagalongs. As soon as we were seated, they started in again. One would point out a woman somewhere in the room, and the other would give an evaluation of her looks. I tolerated the running commentary—but Chuck wasn't seeing it that way. He finally slammed his fist on the table and said to them, "I mean it! Zip those lips. Not another peep until we finish our dinner. And don't look at me. Just sit there. Eat. For Pete's sake, just shut up for a minute!"

"Don't have to tell us twice, Sir" Sims said.

"Consider us zipped." Jones agreed.

Chuck turned to me. "Now tell me more about you. Where did you grow up?"

I had just started to reply when Sims and Jones were at it again, this time whistling as a tall, blonde woman passed by our table.

I looked at Chuck and laughed. He let his mouth fall open, gently slapped himself on the head, and said, "I give up. Let's order some fish. Maybe they'll shut up if their mouths are full."

They didn't.

Chuck ordered the specialty of the house for all of us: red snapper and a popular local side dish of jollof rice topped with slices of a dark-green vegetable called snake gourd, which tasted very much like summer squash. I thought it was all delicious, but Sims and Jones let us know every few minutes it wasn't the steak they were hoping for. And, even with their mouths full, they continued their commentary on just about everything that moved in the café. When one of the cooks walked out of the kitchen area to glance around, Sims saw him and immediately said, "He look sick to you? Looks sick to me. Should we eat this?"

"Reminds me of a cook in a restaurant I know back in Cleveland," Jones chimed in. "Was so sick one night, he gave a disease to half the town. I was one of them!"

At one point, I kicked Chuck under the table and whispered, "Just think of them as our floor show."

The room we were in was breathtaking. Intricately woven tapestries of all colors hung from the walls. Lighted candles inside gleaming brass holders were spaced evenly between them. The tablecloths were also done up in patterns that closely resembled those on the tapestries. To complete the atmosphere, three torches were clustered together in each corner of the room, and the shadows of their flames danced across the floor. "Magnificent," I said to Chuck, pointing around the room. "Thank you for sharing this with me."

We were finishing our main course when a small group of musicians starting setting up in the large open area toward the back. "Good music every night," Chuck explained. "Usually the latest American songs. I love this."

"Not for me," Sims said, placing his napkin on his plate. "I'm sure there's better things to do around here than listen to a bunch of horn blowers. Sir, with your permission, I think Jones and I will be off. You don't have to worry, though. We'll get back to the base on time. Promise."

I knew he wasn't supposed to let them out of his sight, but Chuck rubbed his chin, studied them up and down, and finally said, "Well, I guess that'd be OK—as long as you *promise* to stay out of trouble and get back before I have to send the MPs to look for you. And no dice games! Can I trust you to do that?"

"Yes, Sir!" Jones replied as both stood and prepared to leave. "Thank you, Sir."

Turning to me, Sims said, "Good luck, Lieutenant." He winked, and both were gone.

"Whatever did he mean by that?" Chuck asked, watching them point to and comment about other patrons as they made their way to the door.

I stifled a smile as I said, "I think they were talking about how much I love to dance—that they hoped I'd get the chance tonight. Looks like they're getting an area cleared for that. Do you like to dance?"

"I will with you," he said, taking my hand under the table. "I'm hoping for at least a couple slow songs."

"I might enjoy that, too," I said, squeezing his hand.

∾

Chuck had been right. The orchestra played one current song after another as the dance floor filled up. During the first few songs, we stayed at the table and talked about everything from our childhoods to what we'd been doing back home before the war. He had a wonderful way of telling stories, animating them with hand gestures and different pitches for his voice. And most of his tales were quite funny, punctuated by a perfectly timed dry sense of humor. I could have listened to him all night, but as soon as the orchestra started playing a song he recognized but I didn't, he stood, took my hand, and said, "A dance, please?"

The song had a slow, smooth rhythm, so he held me close as we moved across the floor. I put my head on his shoulder and drew myself in tighter. I didn't want the song to end—the night to end. I tried my best not to think about when or if I was ever going to see him again.

The song ended, and we joined the others on the floor in

a rousing round of applause for the orchestra. "Again?" Chuck asked, as another song started. I nodded my approval, but before we could start moving, there they were, just behind Chuck. Sims and Jones.

"Lieutenants!" Sims called out from the edge of the dance floor. "Got to see you—now!"

His expression was so serious we immediately started making our way toward him, dodging the other dancers as we did so.

"What is it? What's wrong?" I asked, afraid of what his reply might be.

"You've got to come with us!" he replied, his eyes lighting up. "Bet you've never seen anything like it. You'll love it!"

Now, he was smiling broadly.

"What is this?" Chuck asked, gruffly. "You got us off the dance floor for what? This better be good."

"It is!" Jones piped in. "Wait 'till you see it!"

"Enough!" I said, holding up my hand. "OK, what gives? Explain yourselves."

Sims motioned for us to get closer as he said, "The wrestling matches! Just a couple streets over. Biggest goons you've ever seen inside the ropes. Monsters, all of them. Huge! And they whack the tar out of each other. And you can bet on them, too! Sure beats hanging around this joint."

I thought Chuck was going to knock their heads together—and I don't think I'd have blamed him if he did. But, before he could do or say anything, Jones took over. "Please, Sirs! Come with us. We promise you'll love it."

They were like two kids pleading for a bowl of ice cream. Their expressions so pitiful, I started laughing. I finally said, "Well, maybe we should go at that."

"Oh, no you don't," Chuck said, waving a hand in front of me. "You've got to be kidding. I've heard about these places. I don't think we're even supposed to go in them."

Sims cut him off. "Sir, half the base must be there. It's OK. Really."

Chuck looked at me as if hoping I'd throw water on the idea, but it actually sounded fun. Plus, I was feeling moony, sad at the thought of how little time we still had together. I was also afraid those feelings were starting to show, so maybe a quick change of scene might be good for at least a little while.

I also remembered how my father had taken me to a few wrestling matches back in Jersey City when I was a little girl and how I always enjoyed watching Dad and his friends jumping and shouting during the bouts. Looking at Sims and Jones, I could only imagine how they'd react once the action got going.

"Oh, let's go—but just for a minute," I said. "Then it's back here for dancing—and you two aren't to come back with us, understand?"

My response made them positively giddy. Chuck looked at me and shook his head. But, I also saw a little bit of a smile, so I guessed he secretly didn't mind us going all that much. I'd never yet known a man who didn't like the fights or a good wrestling match.

"Show us the way," I said, waving them ahead of us. "Wrestling, here we come!"

~

If I had known where the matches were held, I'd never have agreed to come. Sims had told the truth when he said we had to walk just a couple blocks over from the café, but what he failed to mention was the event was taking place in an old, rundown warehouse that looked like it could fall down at any minute. Even worse, locals with rifles and bullet belts strapped across their shoulders were stationed at both sides of the doors.

"I don't know about this," Chuck said, as we drew closer.

Sims replied, "Come on—live a little, Lieutenant. We'll protect you."

"You, protect, me? Weren't you the ones who took care of everything so well you were going to be shot? You're not making me feel any better."

"Oh, let's go in," I said. "How bad can it be? And I think it'll be fun."

Sims and Jones were right about something. Soldiers were everywhere—to the point they easily outnumbered the locals. However, I didn't see any other officers, so I suggested we stay near the back out of the view of most of the others in the room. Circular rows of tiered seats formed rings that ran from the wrestling area all the way up to the top of the outer walls, providing a good view for each seat. Sims and Jones wanted to sit close, but I kept urging them up the steps until we were almost at the top row.

A match was already in progress as we sat down. But, no sooner were we seated when Sims and Jones jumped back up and started screaming encouragement to the wrestlers. "Which one are they rooting for?" I leaned over and asked Chuck.

"Who knows," he yelled back over the roar of the crowd. "Probably both. I think they're just wound up."

Two huge men slowly circled and slapped at each other in the ring. One must have weighed in at nearly three hundred pounds. He was dark-skinned with a contrasting yellowish, jagged scar running from his ear down to his chin. The other was thinner, but not by much, and a head taller. This one had a much longer reach, so he landed a lot more slaps than his opponent. Suddenly, the taller one lunged forward, grabbed the other's head, and brought his knee up high, catching him flush at the chin. The heavier one toppled back against the ropes, shook his head rapidly back and forth a few times, and charged across the ring, ramming his head into the other's stomach, which caused his tall opponent to lose his balance and flop backward and hard to the ground. The crowd roared its approval as fists were thrust into the air, many of which were waving money. In an instant, the heavier one followed up by jumping into the air and crashing down with full force on the other's stomach. The trapped one winced in pain and tried to roll to the side, but the heavier one continued to press down on him until the official in the ring slapped the ground three times. The cheers rang out again at the same time feet stomped the floor. The combined effect made it feel like the building was shaking, which, given its appearance, was entirely possible. I grabbed Chuck's arm and held tightly.

"Seen enough?" I could barely hear him ask over the still thunderous applause. "Want to get out of here?"

"Just one more!" I yelled to make sure he could hear me. I smiled. "Then back to dancing!"

He laughed, put his arm around me, and held me close just as Sims and Jones started sliding by us toward the aisle. "We'll make a bet for you," Sims said to me. "Which one you like?"

The next two combatants were already in the ring, preparing themselves by stretching and punching themselves all up and down their abdomens. Both were very large men without an obvious difference in their physiques. "I'll take the one with the blue shorts," I said, going with my favorite color. Chuck looked at me and shook his head.

For the next few minutes, each of the wrestlers swung himself back and forth on the ring's ropes, stretched out arm and leg muscles in every way I could think of, and glared and growled at his opponent. While this was still taking place, Sims and Jones came back and slid past us to their seats. "Got you down for a two-dollar bet," Sims said, beaming. "Root him on!"

The official walked back in the ring and called the men together, motioning for them to shake hands. After they had done so, the roar of the crowd increased again as the match started. This time there was no slapping. They got right to business, crashing together and toppling to the floor. They rolled back and forth, each trying to right himself and take control. When they were in the corner closest to us, my wrestler's opponent grabbed him around the neck and started choking him. Some loud boos rang out, but most of those present whooped and howled their approval.

Suddenly, my man slapped his right hand on the floor three times, and the other rolled off him, raising his hand victoriously and screaming loudly while still on the ground. "Sorry," Sims shouted toward me. He tore up two slips of paper and threw them in the air. "Two bucks down the drain."

When I looked back at the ring, my man was still on the ground and clutching at his throat. Even from where we were seated, I could see he was in trouble. "Come on!" I shouted to Chuck just as the applause started slowing. I made my way as quickly as I could down the steps and into the ring, where a small group of men were already kneeling around him. His color was fading as he gasped for breath, clawing frantically at his throat. I instantly knew what had happened and knew what needed to be done.

"Who's got a jackknife?" I shouted, holding out my hand. "Quickly!"

Chuck, standing directly behind me, asked, "What are you doing?"

"Trying to save his life," I said, prying open the man's mouth and placing my index finger as far down his throat as far as I could reach. "His airway's crushed. He'll suffocate." Looking around me, I screamed, "Who's got a knife! I want it, now!"

I couldn't see who thrust it forward, but a thin, single-bladed knife was placed in my hand. "OK, I said to those kneeling around me, I want you to push on his arms and legs so he can't raise up. Do it now!"

When they were in place and had him pinned securely, I looked down and saw his eyes start to roll back as his shaking lessened considerably. "It's now or never," I said, running my hand up and down his neck until I found his Adam's Apple and the thin ridge of cricoid cartilage just below it. Placing the tip of the knife half way between them, I pressed hard enough to cut a slit about a half inch across and half inch deep, exposing the yellow, cricothyroid membrane. I applied even more pressure until I was through the membrane enough to stick my index finger into his airway.

The room had grown absolutely still, so I raised my voice only slightly as I called out, "I need a cigarette holder! A long one! Now!"

Almost instantly, one was passed forward with a lighted cigarette still attached. I flicked that off, blew through the holder to make sure it wasn't plugged, and poked it through the membrane until it was inserted a good two inches. I bent down, sucked until I was sure I was withdrawing air, and then blew through the holder four times in rapid succession.

The man shook violently and tried to rise up, the best sign I could have hoped for. He was getting oxygen again, and color quickly returned to his face. He coughed twice and then eased back to the floor, his chest rising and falling rhythmically. He was out of danger—for now.

A tall man standing next to me had a sash tied around his waist. "I need that!" I commanded, pointing to it. "Take it off."

Without expression, he removed it and handed it to me. I wrapped it snugly around the man's neck to keep the cigarette holder securely in place. The man looked up at me and tried to speak. "Shhh!" I said. "Don't try to talk. You'll be good as new in no time. Don't worry."

I stood and said, to no one in particular, "Get him to a doctor. That's all I can do here."

When no one moved, I repeated it, loudly this time. Finally, the wrestler who was victorious in the first match stepped forward, picked him up, cradled him in his arms, and said, "Hospital." That's all he said. Two other men followed him as he made his way toward the main door.

As soon as they were out of sight, applause started up, slowly at first, then as loudly as I'd heard it before. This was followed by a cascade of coins and bills being tossed into the ring.

"That's for you!" Sims said, suddenly appearing to my right. "I'll scoop it up." Jones joined him, and they soon had bills sticking out from all of their pockets, both pants and shirts. I didn't know what to do, so I just stood there and looked around the room. Everyone was standing and cheering.

"Take a bow," Chuck leaned over and said. "And then let's get the heck out of here."

As I did, the building shook again. Chuck grabbed my arm, and we quickly climbed out of the ring.

$\approx$

"That was some pretty incredible work you did in there," Chuck said once we were outside and on our way back toward the café. "I've never seen anything like that. Isn't that what they call a 'track' something?" You were wonderful."

"Tracheotomy. That's what it's called, and that was about the most unsterile and worst conditions I could have asked for to do it. I'm relieved it worked out OK—at least so far, I guess. I hope they get that man to a doctor pretty quick."

I stopped walking. "Just look at these hands. Caked with blood. And on my shoes, too. I'm a mess!"

Chuck handed me his handkerchief. "Use this. We'll find a spigot somewhere along here. Doesn't bother me at all. You were *amazing*. How'd you know how to do it? That was just so . . . so incredible. You saved his life. He'd be dead now."

"It's not that big of a deal. I've seen it done twice before, so I had a pretty good idea what to do. Still, I could also have killed him. Glad I didn't think about that at the time. I might have chickened out."

"No, you wouldn't have," Chuck said, smiling. "Not you."

A few moments later, he pointed near the back door of a small building. "There's a spigot right over there. I'll wait. Take your time."

After I did my best to clean up, we walked along in silence, hand in hand, until he slid his arm around me. I moved myself even closer, snuggling my head against his shoulder.

About a block farther along he stopped and said, "Say, I just thought of something. Maybe I should marry you for your fortune. I've also never seen it rain down money before. How much do you think you got for helping him?"

"That was a first for me, too," I said, laughing with him. "I have no idea because Sims and Jones pocketed everything. And you know what? I'm just going to let them keep it. They'd probably just steal it later anyway. No, I don't want the money. They can have it."

"You're really are something, Lieutenant. Something very special."

As we rounded the corner at the main road, we saw the line of people outside the café door was nearly all the way back to us. "Well, that takes care of that," I said, my heart sinking.

Chuck squeezed my arm. "It's getting late anyway. We better head back. Let's see if we can flag a taxi."

"What about Sims and Jones?" I asked, looking behind us.

"What about them? Let's worry about only ourselves for now."

The taxi ride back was quick and without incident, so we soon found ourselves seated on a long, wooden bench just to the left of the main hospital entrance. The fullness of the moment hit me hard as I started coming to grips with the fact this might be the last time we'd be together for a long time—or ever. There was so much welling up inside me. So much I wanted to say. I also knew there was nothing we could do about the situations we were in. The Army owned us for the duration. That was just a fact, one we had to live with, no matter what was in our hearts. I moved closer to Chuck as he again put his arm around me and drew me to him.

Lifting my chin so I could look into his eyes, he said, gently, "We're not going to do one of those long goodbye scenes like in the movies. There's no need to. Instead, I'm going to say this very plainly."

He reached down and took my hand again. "Look, I'm falling head over heels. There's no other way to say it. I'd give anything on this earth for the circumstances to be different. But they're not. So, here's what I have to say. You are going to be deep in my heart—and that isn't going anywhere. I already know that. Wherever I go, whatever I'm doing, I'll be thinking about you—and about the dreams I have."

Chuck pulled me close and hugged me, and I held tight. After a few moments, he eased me back a little, slowly leaned over, and kissed me. Gently, full on the lips.

"I feel the same," I said when we each drew back. "It's hard for me to put it into words, but I know what I'm feeling. The same will go for me. It doesn't matter one bit where I'll be, you'll be right there at my side."

"Let's not say anything else," he said, brushing back my hair. "Let's keep this in our hearts. Keep it with us always."

After a few quiet moments, he stood up. "I hope I see you again really soon. I'm going to pray for that."

"And me, too," I said, getting up.

We kissed again, this time slowly, passionately. Then, he backed away, turned, waved, and started walking toward the airfield. When he was almost at the end of the sidewalk, he turned and called back, "You take good care of yourself, Boom Boom. You're awfully special to me."

As he walked out of sight, tears streamed down my cheeks.

~

After Chuck had gone, I decided to go in and check on the men one more time. All were asleep when I entered the room, even Sam. There was an open bed over by the window, so I took off my shoes and walked quietly over. I was so tired, so ready to close my eyes. I pulled back one of the thin sheets, crawled in, covered myself up, and was out like a light.

However, I wasn't destined for good sleep this night. Just after midnight I felt my shoulders being shaken, violently. "Wake up! Wake up!" a familiar voice shouted.

When the rest of the room lights were switched on, I saw it was Chuck before me.

"What in the world are you doing here?" I asked, still startled, sitting right up.

"Your new crew sent me over to get all of you ready to go. They've been ordered to leave right now because the weather forecast over the Atlantic is horrible. If you don't go now, you'd be trapped here at least a couple days. No time to waste. A truck is already down by the entrance. Do what you need to do—and get everybody rolling."

Sam and I had now done this so many times it took just over ten minutes to have everyone outside and aboard the truck. Chuck rode up front with the driver so he could direct him the fastest route to the plane. Once we got there, again because of our newly-gained experience, it didn't take long to have everyone settled in place. However, there were two main obstacles we immediately had to deal with. The first was the fact the Seabees were everywhere inside the plane, including the rear section that had been reserved for us. We knew they were along for the ride, but they hadn't been told anything about us. Once the real estate situation had been cleared up, the other problem was how to get the stretchers down in the bomb bay section without jostling and hurting the men on them. That, too, was solved quickly when four of the burliest Seabees came forward and easily and gently lowered the stretchers. Everything else fell right into place.

"All ready to go!" I finally shouted toward the cockpit. At that moment, I looked across from me and saw Chuck buckled into a seat. I had momentarily forgotten about him in all the commotion.

"Where do you think you're going?" I asked, utterly confused.

"Honestly," he said, "I didn't know until I got back to our ship, but Jordan told me that the orders had come down while we were out tonight. I'm being sent along with you. At least as far as Morrison Field in Florida. So, it looks like it's not going to be easy to get rid of me."

I was just about to tell him how happy I was when I was tapped on the shoulder from behind. There they were, again. Sims and Jones. "And you get us, too!" Sims said, laughing. "All the way back home!"

Before I could say anything to anybody, the engines of the B-24 roared to life.

∾

Chapter 12

"Why Us?"

0517 ZULU, January 21
(50 miles east of Ascension Island)

ROLLER COASTER.

That kept popping into my head as we shook, bounced, rattled, and often suddenly dropped altitude. It didn't help that nearly all the Seabees were gagging and coughing and filling buckets and cups with what little remained in their stomachs. If we had truly "beat the storms" by leaving Accra early, I'd have hated to see what really bad weather would have been like.

At the same time, the new ship took some getting used to. I was told it would be a lot smoother than a C-47, but this leg of the journey made that terribly difficult for me to believe. It was, however, larger in almost every respect. The B-24 had four engines, which made it move at over twice the speed of the *Able Mabel*. It could also fly at a much higher altitude, providing an extra layer of security as that made it more difficult for the enemy to spot. The interior was a good half again larger than the C-47 because the B-24 had been built as a bomber and needed the extra space for weapons. The only real drawback I could see from the standpoint of moving patients was fewer windows, which caused our section of the ship to be quite dark and seem closed-in. But, the converted bomb bay section provided a much more secure way of transporting those on stretchers, and for that I was grateful—especially while watching Lieutenant Collins and Private Montague ride out the bumps.

Shortly after we were airborne, Chuck moved up with the crew. I had met our pilot and co-pilot the day before, but I still hadn't been introduced to the navigator. Sam said the B-24 normally had a much larger crew, but because this ship had been switched to courier service, the three-man crew would be sufficient. While looking toward the cockpit, it dawned on me we had been forced to leave Accra so quickly I didn't get a chance to thank and say goodbye to Lieutenants Jordan and Dix. I had so much I wanted to say to them. Now all I could do was hope they'd stay safe and our paths would cross again in the future.

Because we were bouncing around so much, we had to spend most of time keeping the men calm and securely in place, not easy tasks to do with all the retching coming from our Seabees. However, Sims and Jones stepped in and actually helped out a great deal by sharing their tales of adventure with anyone who would listen. Their words were a nice contrast to the lightning that seemed to crack closer and closer to the wings of the ship as we rolled along. I was proud of them and happy for their assistance. However, at one point during the only smooth stretch we had, I looked around and couldn't find them. That is, I couldn't until I looked toward the front of the ship and saw they were kneeling down and playing dice with a group of the Seabees. By the yowls I heard coming from that direction, I could guess what was happening.

I couldn't say I saw anyone who appeared calm during our roller coaster ride—I certainly wasn't—but eventually there became something of a rhythm and routine to the sudden jolts of movement. Sims and Jones were the most upset of all, but not because of the weather. The jostling up and down made it too difficult to keep track of their dice, so their game with the Seabees had to be suspended. "Would you do me a favor?" I asked, as they sadly made their way back toward us. "Think you could go down there and keep the stretchers in place while Sam and I go over the medical charts?" Sims replied, "Might as well. With all this goin' on, won't be any more action tonight."

Sam and I updated the charts, adding notations related to everything from temperature to pulse rate to general disposition of each man. However, before we could finish, the bouncing increased steadily again until it was impossible to keep our pencils on the paper.

"I give up!" I finally said, snapping a file closed. "I can't do this!"

Sam nodded. "My handwriting on this chart looks like I did too much drinking before writing it. I'm done, too."

We both cinched up our seatbelts as tight as we could stand them and sat. At that point, there wasn't much else we could do.

After one particularly unsettling drop in altitude, Sam looked over at me and asked, "Why us?"

"Just lucky, I guess."

"No, I don't mean this," he said pointing out the rear window. "I mean why you—me. Have you thought at all why we were chosen for this mission? I keep thinking about that, and I'm not sure I like what I've come up with."

"I think we were just handy," I said. "They obviously wanted to start in Karachi for some reason and, well, we were there. And besides, I've been keeping my eye on you, and you're pretty darn good at your work, Liberator. I can't think of anyone else I'd rather have with me right now."

"That's kind of you to say, and I appreciate it. But don't you think a doctor should have been sent along instead of me for something this important? That's part of what's bothering me. I'm not bad with bandages and iodine, but I don't get too much away from that most of the time."

He paused a moment. "Now, I mean this with no disrespect, but I'd like to ask you something if it's OK. We haven't really talked a lot about this, but do you have much family back home waiting for you when the war's over? I've got my family in St. Louis, but there are so many of us I don't think I'd be missed all that much. I'm not saying this well, but do you know what I'm getting at?"

What Sam was suggesting hadn't really occurred to me until then, but I started wondering if he weren't at least partially right. But I didn't get the chance to reply because both of us had our attention stolen by Chuck, who staggered from one handhold to the next on his way back toward us.

"I know this is going to sound like a broken record, but get everything secure," he began, his face dead-serious. "Just got word the strip had a good hammering again late yesterday. We're not sure what exactly we're going to run up against. Might not be pretty."

"Wouldn't expect otherwise," I replied, shaking my head. "If we had a smooth landing, it wouldn't be natural. I think I'd just faint away."

"Me, too," Sam said. "I don't enjoy it now if my teeth aren't rattling when we touch down."

"That's the spirit," Chuck teased. "Get yourselves and the

men situated. We're almost there. I'll yell back when it's time to brace."

Looking down into the bomb bay, he said, "Wouldn't want to be them, though. Their teeth will be rattling for sure."

Chuck returned to the cockpit as Sam and I checked seatbelts and offered encouragement to all, especially Sims and Jones, who were still down in the bomb bay. There weren't many places for them to grab hold to keep themselves in place, so we suggested they start now looking for something, anything, that would help keep them upright.

A few minutes later, Chuck called back, "Two minutes! Hold tight!"

Through the rear window, I could see we were dropping through a bank of low-lying clouds, which caused the ship to shake violently again. Once through, I could see the ground just below us. We were so close I noticed a group of men running from a large tent over to a bright-red truck.

The engines screamed as our nose started rising again at such force I couldn't even tilt my head forward to peer out the window. A few of the Seabees ahead of us loudly and desperately shouted curses and questions.

Our climb continued as we banked hard to the left, so much so that everything I had anchored on the right shelves broke free and shot across the ship. "What in the . . ." was all Sam got out before a can hit him squarely on the neck, causing him to recoil in pain.

A few seconds later, the co-pilot yelled back toward us, "We're fine, now! All is safe! We're just going around again. Couldn't see the damage at the start of the strip until we were right on it. We'll try it again. Hang on!"

A wave of relief instantly washed over most of us. However, the fact that we knew we weren't going to crash also caused some to relax just enough they could throw up. Buckets and cups were again filled, and the smell did nothing to help the rest of us.

The ship continued banking left, but we soon leveled off and started a slow, gradual descent. This time the clouds didn't bump us too much. Our wheels finally touched the ground, and as they did, the Seabees clapped and shouted their thanks. More also threw up.

"Sam, I don't think I'll ever fly again after we get home," I deadpanned. "They better be sending me back by ship or I'm just not going."

"Same with me," he laughed. "Never again. My feet are staying on the ground."

We taxied to a series of Quonset huts, finally stopping near the largest. The minute our doors opened, the Seabees, to a man, grabbed their gear and equipment and raced out of the plane. I thought it was one of the rudest things I'd ever witnessed—until I saw they were dumping their personal gear by the nose of the ship and heading straight for the field to begin repairs. They hadn't even bothered to send a representative to the field command to announce their arrival. In a matter of seconds, they were driving trucks, bulldozers, and jeeps through a heavy rain toward the areas of damage.

"Look at 'em go!" Sam said, slapping his leg. "Sure hope they get finished before we have to leave."

So did I.

There was only a small first-aid station, so we kept the men aboard the ship while it was refueled and checked over. Sam stayed with the patients while I went off to see about getting some breakfast for everybody.

As I suspected, Headquarters was inside the largest Quonset hut, and a very polite orderly there directed me to head three huts down, where the mess was located. I had just started that way when I saw Chuck.

"I'm still mad at you!" I said, sternly, but my smile betrayed me. "If I had known last night wasn't goodbye..."

"I already explained that," he said, raising his arms. "Honestly, I didn't know any of this myself until I got back to our ship last night—after I left you. I swear that's the truth."

Folding my arms, I asked, "So, just what in the world are you doing here?"

He laughed. "My story isn't as secret as whatever you've got going on. I can at least tell you some of it, I guess. My transfer orders caught up with me. I'll tell you more about that later. I needed a ride back to the States as part of that, so I suggested I be allowed to join up with all of you. That was granted, and here I am."

"Oh, you're not getting off that easy," I scolded him. "I want details—and lots of them. I want to know everything."

He reached over, gently squeezed my arm, and started bending down to kiss me. Several men were walking toward us, so I cleared my throat and said, teasing him again, "Not until I hear the rest. Don't know if you deserve it."

"Fair enough," he replied. "At least how about some breakfast? I'm starved."

"My goodness!" I said, slapping my forehead. "I'm supposed to be getting some for the men—and Sam."

"Then I'll help you with that. I'm not needed for anything else right now. Let's see what we can round up."

"The mess is over there. Get going, Lieutenant!"

Because of the recent attacks, cooking had fallen to a very low priority. All we could come up with were some rock-hard biscuits, a jug of cold coffee, and a tray of fruit that had seen much better days. Still, it was better than nothing, and we were glad to have it. Chuck, good to his word, helped serve the men and did his best to raise their spirits. I think they were grateful for a familiar face and someone to talk to other than Sam and me.

When we finished, Sam took over again while we went back to headquarters to see if there was any news about when we'd be able to leave. A large section of headquarters had been partitioned off to form a meeting area, and that is where we found most of the base officers huddled around a radio, struggling to hear some news of the war through the loud, crackling static.

A major who had just walked in asked, to no one in particular, "Well, anything? Anything at all?"

"Nothing about what's happening to us, if that's what you mean," a young lieutenant replied. "But, earlier, I did hear a report that said the British knocked the snot out of the Italians and Germans day before yesterday up at a place called Zuwarah, somewhere on the North African coast. Guess they wiped out the Italian navy there and a mess of German fighters. They're saying that might shove 'em out of Africa totally. I sure hope so. About time."

"So that's why . . ." I started to say, catching myself and stopping. Chuck looked at me and put a finger to his lips. I knew he was thinking the same thing: that the German fighter we had encountered most likely had been in that area because of that offensive.

Just then the static cleared, and an announcement came through crystal clear.

On the 17th, the German Luftwaffe resumed nighttime bombing of London for the first time in nearly a year. Yesterday, a daring daylight raid resulted in many more civilian targets being hit, including a school where forty-one children and six of their schoolmasters were killed. The German bombers had somehow broken through without warning, resulting in this terrible tragedy. More details will be forthcoming.

While listening to the broadcast, I realized what I had been going through was nothing I should be complaining about. We all had to do our part and let the chips fall where they may. That was all we could do. That was all we should do. Some of us weren't going to get home. I knew that. I hoped it wouldn't be me, but what we were fighting for was greater than any individual. That was a tough realization to come to, a sobering thought I tried not to think about. But, when I heard about the London bombings and those poor children, all came flooding back.

The young lieutenant shouted, "Lousy, stinkin' . . . Children! Children!" He reached over and turned off the radio. We all stood there a moment in silence before turning to leave.

Lieutenant Forbes came toward us, and Chuck said, "Elsie, have you met Forbes, our pilot?"

He and I smiled at each other as I said, "Why, of course. He and I are old pals, right?"

Lieutenant Forbes replied, "That's right. From way back." Looking at his watch, he added, "Looks like we're going to be here a little longer. I hope just an hour or so. They're working pretty hard on the field, bless them. I think in the meantime I'll grab a bite. You two want anything?"

"No," I replied. "We're good. Please just let us know as soon as you can when we'll be leaving. I'd like a little notice to make sure the men are prepared."

As soon as he had gone, Chuck said to me, "Way back? How do you know him?"

"Oh, I get around," I teased. "You'd be surprised."

"Well, I've got a few surprises of my own," he said, motioning for me to follow him to a bench over by the walkway across from headquarters.

When we were seated, he said, while taking off his hat. "I can't say much because I don't really know too many details, but here is what I do know." He shifted more toward me. "A few months back I heard they were looking for pilots for a new type of squadron they're going to try in the Pacific. I thought I could help out more by having my own ship, so I put in for a transfer for that. I don't know where I'm being sent for training. I'm supposed to get to Morrison Field, and instructions will be waiting for me there. That's the whole story. All I know for now."

"It's admirable, what you did," I said, moving closer. "But, it also sounds dangerous. And, too far away . . . from *me*." I looked around to make sure no one was looking and took his hand.

"I just felt I needed to do it."

"I know. I don't like it, but I understand. Some of it anyway."

"And what about you? What happens after this? Where do you think you'll be sent?"

"Back to Karachi, I guess. Don't really know. To tell the truth, I don't have any idea what they plan for me."

He leaned closer as if getting ready to kiss me, but a group of soldiers came out of the mess and started walking by.

"Well, let's just wish for the best," he said, irritated by the interruption. "For both of us."

We had so much more to day but stopped when one of the Seabees ran up to us. "Quick! The Sergeant sent me to find you. Wants you back at the ship pronto!"

"I better go see," I said, letting go of Chuck's hand. "What now?"

"I'll go with you," he said. "Let's go!"

When we got back to the ship, we climbed in as quickly as we could. As soon as Sam saw me, he said, "Thank goodness! He's over there." He pointed to Corporal Ernst, who was huddled in the back against the gun turret compartment. "Can't get him to stop screaming and crying. At first I thought he was saying he was hot, that he was burning up. But I realized he wasn't saying he was hot—he was asking for you. He kept calling out, 'Ott, Ott, Ott!' He wants you."

Corporal Ernst, his arms wrapped tightly around his chest, was rocking back and forth violently side to side. He finally looked up, saw me, and immediately changed the rocking so that he was moving rhythmically forward and back. He looked up again, opened his mouth as if he were trying to say something, and burst into tears, his body wracked by the sobs.

Trying not to startle him, I began taking very small steps toward him. Once I was directly before him, I slowly knelt down, smiled, and kept myself absolutely still. His rocking continued as the cries grew louder. I scooted forward, raised my right hand, and placed it gently on his left shoulder when he next rocked toward me. Doing so allowed me to keep contact and rock back and forth with him. When he finally looked up and our eyes met, he stopped rocking, leaned forward, reached out, and hugged me, tightly.

"Shhhh!" I said, patting him on the back. "It's all right."

His voice hoarse, raspy, he softly repeated over and over, "Home. Home. Home."

It was the only word I'd heard him say the whole journey.

"I know," I said as reassuringly as I could. "Me, too. I understand."

Less than a minute later, he sat back, dabbed his eyes, and nodded to me. Without saying anything else, he reached for a blanket, covered himself, and lay back, closing his eyes as he did. I didn't expect him to say any more.

∼

Exactly an hour and ten minutes later, the field had been worked enough we were in the air and on our way again, this time less eleven Seabees. However, Sims and Jones more than made up for the Seabees' absence by regaling us with the story of how they had managed in a very short amount of time to part the Seabees from most of their money. When I suggested perhaps that happened because the dice they were using were loaded, Sims drew back, let his mouth fall open, and said, "Who? Us? Lieutenant, I'm shocked—shocked you would even think that."

Jones laughed—until Sims smacked him on the side of his head and said, "What are you laughing at?"

We all howled.

The next leg of our journey seemed to go quickly because we finally flew out of the storms. The flight became smooth, the purr of the engines rhythmic and steady.

However, right after I checked the men once again and the pilot announced we were about twenty minutes from Natal, Brazil, my temples started throbbing unlike anything I'd ever experienced before while suffering a headache. I kept getting short spells of dizziness. My stomach began hurting, followed by a wave of nausea.

"You OK?" Sam asked, stepping forward and grabbing my arm. "You're . . . You're bleeding. Out your nose . . ."

"What? Where?" I asked, growing dizzier by the second.

I reached for him to steady myself, and all went black.

~

Chapter 13

Roadblocks

1620 ZULU, January 21
Natal, Brazil

WHEN I OPENED MY EYES, I had an oxygen mask covering my face, and a doctor was using a stethoscope to check my heart.

"Where am I? Where are we?" I asked, startled. I ripped off the mask and tried to sit up.

"We're at Natal," Chuck said, gently pushing me back down. "You scared us to death! All of a sudden, you just flopped down."

"I'm OK. Really!" I said, pushing the doctor back. As my mind started to clear, I realized I was on a cot just outside the cargo door. "I think I just lost my balance is all."

"What you did was lose your chow. All over the place!" Jones said, moving toward me. "What a mess."

Sims smacked him hard on the arm and shoved him back. I looked to the side and saw Sam and the crew circling me from that direction. Behind them, I could see Captain Goldman and Private Scalini.

The doctor started laughing. "What is this? Your personal harem? You sure have a lot of men worried about you."

I didn't answer him. Instead, I repeated, "I tell you I'm fine.

Nothing wrong with me that a little walking around won't cure. Let me up!"

"Not quite yet," the doctor scolded, pressing against my arm. "What you've got is a classic case of altitude sickness. Keep sucking that oxygen a few minutes, and take two of these tablets. I think you'll be fine, but I'm sending along a small tank of oxygen in case you start feeling woozy again. This part of the world requires flying higher than most places you'll ever go, so I want you to be prepared."

Chuck knelt down next to me. "The doc said he'd rather you spend the night here to give you a little recovery time. We can do that if you want."

"I most certainly do not want!" I shot back. "I'm fine. Fine. Just give me a minute, and we can take off again. Sam, how are the rest of the men? Are they well?"

Sam stepped through the gathered group and replied, "Better than you are. That's for sure."

That brought a nice round of laughter from everyone—myself included. "Ok, that's enough," I said, waving all of them back. "Do what you need to do to the plane. Give me a couple of minutes to walk around. Then, let's get going. We've got to stay on schedule. I'm telling you—I'm *fine!*"

Jones spoke up, "Anyone that bossy has to be fine. I think she'll be ok."

"Thank you, *doctor,*" Sims said, whacking Jones so hard he started running toward the plane. The others laughed again and followed him.

∾

Twenty minutes later we were in the air again. Thankfully, the flight was smooth, which helped me tremendously. I didn't let on to anyone, but my stomach was still queasy, and at times I found it hard to catch my breath, especially after walking up and down the aisle.

We kept flying overnight, making just two other stops, at Belem, Brazil, and Borinquen, Puerto Rico. Everyone but Chuck and the crew stayed on the ship both places. At Borinquen, while the refueling and safety checks took place, Chuck managed to get us some bananas and freshly baked bread. We were all so hungry, we felt like we had been given a feast.

As we continued through the night, Sam and I alternated checking on the men and taking naps. Chuck came back once to check on me and make sure the altitude illness was behind me, but other than that, he stayed forward with the crew.

Finally, just before noon, I could feel the ship start a deliberate and steady descent. It wasn't long after that, Chuck walked back toward us.

"Won't be long now," he beamed. "We'll be on U.S. soil in about twenty minutes. Morrison Field is dead ahead. It's going to be so good to be home!"

Shortly after, just as our wheels touched the ground, everyone but Corporal Ernst erupted in applause and cheers. Corporal Ernst just stared out the window, but I could tell by the way he placed his hand on the glass, he, too, was glad to be back.

While we taxied in, I asked Sam to make the arrangements to have the men put up for the night at the base hospital, so I could have a few minutes alone with Chuck before he had to leave. But, it turned out Chuck had already asked the crew to radio ahead to have medical personnel standing by. As soon as we stopped, trucks were waiting for us. Sam climbed out first so he could supervise everything.

As he was doing that, I motioned for Chuck to follow me over toward a hanger just to our right. When we were out of earshot of the others, I turned and said, "Now, I've already said my goodbyes once, so I'm going to make this quick."

"Quick?" he asked, looking around before drawing me toward him. "I don't think so."

He leaned forward and kissed me, gently, and pulled me closer. "I have the feeling this is going to have to last a while," he added, placing his arms around me. This time I kissed him back, hard, wrapping my arms around him as tightly as I could.

"I don't want any more goodbyes," I said, stepping back. "My heart can't take it."

"We won't say that. 'Until we meet again' is better—and I want that very much. Elsie, you've got to promise me you'll write as often as you can—and I'll do the same—so we can share everything about ourselves. I want you to know me—to know what you're getting into."

"I think I might like that," I said, kissing him gently. "And I promise. At least a letter every week, no matter where I am or what I'm doing. I'll always make that time for you."

I felt the tears welling up. "Now, none of that," he said, lifting up my chin. "My heart's the same, and you'll always be there."

"You better go," I said, wiping my eyes. "And I need to find Sam . . ."

Before I could say anything else, he leaned down and kissed me once again. Stepping back, he pointed to Sims and Jones, who were seated on the running board of a car and smiling at us.

"My shadows," Chuck said, dryly. "I'm supposed to take them with me when I report here—probably to make sure they actually get to the office." He shook his head. "Just look at those two. What a pair!"

"Oh, go on!" I said, ushering him forward. "You better get out of here before *I* go with you, too!"

"You don't know how much I wish you could," he said. "You take care, Boom Boom. And keep me in your heart."

I quickly walked away so he couldn't see the tears.

I was a few yards from the plane when the pilot climbed out and ran over to me. "There you are!" he said. "Thank goodness! I looked around a few minutes ago and couldn't find you anywhere. We got new orders. I'm not sure why, but we leave again in thirty minutes—this time without you. Some kind of emergency is all I can gather. They asked for us specifically. I'm sorry, but it looks like you're on your own now."

"What do you mean?" I asked, at first thinking he was joking with me until I saw how serious his expression was becoming. "This can't be!"

"Again, I'm sorry," he said. "We're rushing the fueling right now and getting the new charts ready. There will be barely enough time to get your supplies off. See that truck back there. I got it right away when we heard the news. You might want to go over and check on it. I've got to get back on board and get us ready. Sorry, Lieutenant. Good luck."

With that, he was gone.

I was still so stunned I didn't move for a minute. "No plane?" I said aloud. "What are we going to do?"

The first thought was to rush to the Field Operations office to see if anyone there could suggest something to help us out. However, before I had a chance to do anything, Sam came running up, so out of breath he had to stand in front of me several seconds before he could speak.

"Well," I said, growing impatient. "While you're winding yourself back up, get a load of this. Our pilot just told me they have to take off right away, so we can't go with them tomorrow morning."

I pointed to the truck next to the plane. "They're unloading us now. Look at that. What in the world are we going to do, Sam?"

He finally settled down enough to speak, but his words still came rapidly. "I can go one better than that," he said, the disgust obvious. "We might not need a plane anyway because the hospital administrator just told me he's keeping the men. He said this is the end of the line as far as you and I are concerned. He feels it's in *our* patients' best interest to be admitted and evaluated here—and then sent wherever the best treatment is for them."

Before I could get a word in, he said, "Elsie, I don't like this man. I told him we were on a special mission—that we had to get everyone to Walter Reed. When I said that, he just laughed at me. Laughed at me. You better get over there and see what you can do with him. If we can't get the men back, nothing else is going to matter. We'll be cooked, and I think I know what that would mean for you. So, while you look into that, what can I do? Name it."

When I finally had a chance to speak, I said, "He can't do that! He doesn't have the authority. I've still got the letter right here. I'll show him!"

Drawing out each word slowly, I repeated, "He doesn't have the authority."

"He sure *thinks* he does," Sam replied, shaking his head.

"He's got another think coming. Where's his office?"

"Main floor—right in the middle. Good luck. I think you—*we're*—going to need it."

∾

When I entered the office and introduced myself, the clerk told me the acting chief administrator, Doctor Adams, was busy, and I'd have to sit in a chair over by the window and wait.

"This is important," I said, placing my hands on the clerk's desk. "Please announce me at once. I need to see him as soon as possible. It's about the men I just brought here. I have to tell him something about them."

"Again," the clerk said, "you'll just have to wait your turn. Doctor Adams has a lot of business to take care of today. But, I'm sure it won't be long."

"Please," I implored, lowering my voice. "Please announce me. I'd consider it a great favor."

Without replying to me, the clerk shook his head slowly and walked to the administrator's door. He opened it wide enough I had a good view inside. I saw the doctor sitting at his desk, but I didn't see anyone else in there with him. The clerk finally said. "There's some nurse out here who wants to see you about men she says she just brought here. Says she wants to see you right away."

I couldn't hear the doctor's reply. The clerk closed the door, walked back to his desk, and sat down without saying anything to me.

"Well?" I asked. "What did he say?"

"You'll just have to wait," he said without looking up. "He'll call you when he's ready."

I waited. And waited. And waited some more. I finally checked my watch. Fifteen minutes had gone by. Then twenty. Then thirty. When it got to forty-five minutes, I stood up and started pacing back and forth in front of the clerk's desk, hoping he'd be so bothered he'd check again to see if I could go in. However, I didn't faze him. He kept right at his work, as if I wasn't even there.

Finally, the door opened and Doctor Adams motioned for me to follow him in. As soon as we were seated, I handed him the letter and told him how I had been ordered not to let anything stand in my way while completing the mission—that I had been told to expect full cooperation at every stop. I explained I had to be at Walter Reed the next day—and I'd appreciate any help he could provide. I purposely kept talking so that he couldn't respond until I'd had my say. Finally, I asked if he'd make sure the men were looked over right away and gotten ready for the last part of our journey.

At that point, his face turned beet-red. He cut me off by pounding a fist on his desk and saying, loudly, "Just who do you think you are! I'm not one of your Army docs, so I don't have to pay attention to anything this says."

He threw the letter roughly on his desk. "I can't be forced around. I'm filling in for the Head Administrator here, as a favor while everyone's at a medical conference. I was told to use my own best judgment in every situation. And right now, that tells me to keep those patients here where they can get the proper care they need."

He paused, sucked in a deep breath, and continued. "How dare you try to tell me what I need to do. You're just a . . . a nurse, after all. You're not a doctor. You don't know what's best. And don't you try to tell me you do, Missy. Now you get out of here. This discussion has ended. They're staying here! Right here! You, go!"

He stood, walked to the window, turned his back to me, and stared out.

"But, Sir!" was all I got out before he whirled around and shouted, "Get out of my office!"

I was so stunned I didn't know how to respond. Clearly, nothing I could say was going to help, so I got up and slowly walked out into the hallway, my mind racing a mile a minute. I walked up the flight of steps to the floor where Sam had said the men were being kept and saw a folding chair in the hallway outside their door. I walked over to it and sat down. I was still fuming, hopping mad, like I hadn't felt in years—maybe ever. But, as fast as my mind was racing, I still remembered something I had learned a long time ago: anything worth doing is worth fighting for. And now, more than ever, I wasn't going to lie down. To the contrary, this was a time to figure out a counterattack. No, I wasn't going to let some civilian administrator get the best of me. Not after everything we'd been through to get this far.

I was still fighting through my anger, trying to come up with my next move, when Sims and Jones rushed down the hallway toward me. "There you are!" Sims shouted. "Been looking all over. Ran into Sergeant Rigazzi. We were helping him take your supplies out of the plane and load them in the truck when he told us everything. Couldn't believe it. This is horrible!"

Before I could respond, Jones said, "You look terrible, Sir. No disrespect intended. You just . . ."

Sims shoved him back and said, "Don't pay any attention to him. And don't you worry any more. I think we can get you out of this. We don't have to leave until tomorrow, so we're sticking with you until everything gets settled. I want you to know you can count on us."

"Thanks," I said, exhaling loudly. "I really appreciate it."

I relayed my conversation with the doctor as best I could, hoping that doing so would help me come up with some ideas. It didn't. Instead, I just grew angrier. Finally, after I started slowing down, Sims interrupted me and said, smiling broadly, "Well, I think we got at least part of the problem taken care of already."

He looked at Jones, then at me, smiled again, and said, "Lieutenant, will a DC-3 do?"

"What do you mean?" I asked standing. "What are you talking about?"

"A plane," he said. "A DC-3, if that's OK. That's the best we could do on short notice. Started working on it as soon as Sergeant Rigazzi filled us in. He said he wanted a miracle. Well, he didn't have to ask for that. You've got us. In a situation like this, we can do better sometimes."

Jones laughed and said, "*Way* better—as long as nobody sees us."

"How? Where?" was all I could get out before Sims continued. "Well, actually, *we* didn't get it. You did."

When he saw my confused expression, he said, "At least your *money* did. Remember your winnings at the wrestling matches? We kept that safe for you, and it's come in handy. Found a jockey who's taking a ship up north for repairs. After a little negotiating, he said he'd take you and your crowd with him in the morning if you can be ready. That's when he has to go. What do you think?"

When he finally let me have a word, I said, "I think you two could be shot for this. You realize that, right?"

Jones smiled and said, "Oh, that's already been tried, and it didn't take. Besides, they can't shoot us now. We're heroes, remember? Don't worry about us. You sure you want to try this? Seems to me you've a lot more to lose than we do."

"Absolutely!" I shot back. "No doubt in my mind."

I reached over, drew them to me, and hugged them both. "Do I want to know how you did this?"

"I don't think so," Sims said, backing away. "Let's just say the wheels have been greased and leave it at that. OK?"

Jones added, "You still have one big problem." He pointed to the room. "How are you going to get 'em out of here and to the plane? That's not going to be easy."

"You let me worry about that. You've done the hard part. I'll think of something. Now, take me to this plane. I need to check out a few things there. But, before we go, there's a supply closet across the hall. How about if we make a stop there on the way out?"

"Lieutenant!" Sims replied. "Now *I'm* the one who's shocked. I think you've been hanging around us too much."

"Or not enough," I said, dryly. "Let's go!"

∾

Chapter 14

"Hold Your Breath"

0851, January 23
Morrison Field, West Palm Beach, Florida

The cool Florida morning felt good on my face and arms—a welcome contrast to the stifling heat of El Fasher and Kano. However, I still felt perspiration forming at my temples and under my arms. It wasn't from the heat, though. It was from the thought that my next actions could end my military service and, possibly, my nursing career.

Here I was, sitting on a bench outside a U.S. Army Base Hospital, getting ready to team up with two men who, less than a week before, had been a few hours from a date with a firing squad. Our plan was going to take misdirection, precision timing, and lots of luck. The thought made me shiver.

Sims and Jones pulled up in a truck and quickly stepped out. Each—courtesy of one more raid of the supply closet—was wearing a long, white orderly coat and had a surgical mask covering most of his face. I could tell it was them because one kept smacking the other, and both talked nonstop.

I wagged a finger at them and clutched my hand to my chest. "I'm already about to have a heart attack," I said, scolding them. "Please, this has to be as serious as death. No more playing around. And no more talking. No talking while we're inside. I'll do all of that. You just stand there and look as somber as you can through those masks. Understood?"

"Sorry, Lieutenant," Sims said. "Just having fun is all. We dropped Sergeant Rigazzi at the ship. He wanted me to tell you he'd make sure all was ready there."

"Good—thanks." I calmed a bit, easing my tone. "Now you keep behind me. Let's do this fast—before anyone has a chance to think about it. I've already gone over everything with the men, so they should be ready. Bless their hearts. They've all agreed to do this so we can get to Walter Reed as planned. Plus, the duty change is just about to start, which means there's going to be commotion everywhere in a couple of minutes. We first have to get by the guards at the side door. Hopefully, after standing there all night, they won't want to stick around, and we're going to play on that. So, are you ready? Let's go scare some people!"

Two guards stood at the side entrance, both very young and appearing quite sleepy, as I'd hoped they would be. We stopped right before them. I handed each a mask and introduced myself, saying my name so quickly I hoped they wouldn't catch it. "I'm Lieutenant Elsie Ott. I'm here to collect the tuberculosis patients and get them to quarantine."

I didn't give them a chance to respond as both looked down at the masks. I shook my head and said, as solemnly as I could, "Poor fellows. One has an active case and gave it to nearly his whole squad before we knew it. Laboratory tests just confirmed it's a particularly nasty and highly contagious form. That's why I gave you masks. When we come back down, make sure you put them on. And, this is most important of all—hold your breath until we're completely by. If you don't, you could be exposed. Any questions?"

"Worst cases I've ever seen," Sims said, shaking his head. "Better do what she says. Wouldn't want you to have to be put in quarantine with the rest. That'd be horrible."

I nodded my agreement, and again without giving the guards time to react, said to Sims and Jones, "Let's get 'em, but be careful. Keep those masks tight, and remember—whatever happens, don't breathe through your mouths."

I waved Sims and Jones along as we entered and started climbing the steps. Once at the top, I looked back down, and the guards were just standing there, staring at the masks.

The hallway on the second floor was beginning to show signs of the duty change. At the other end of the hall I could see the new shift of nurses and orderlies looking at charts and preparing to go into the rooms to check on patients. Fortunately, our men were in the very last room in the south wing. That gave us some extra time, but we still needed to hurry.

As soon as we entered the room, Captain Goldman started coughing, gagging, and pulling at his mask.

"Oh, no! You OK?" I asked.

"Just practicing," he said, laughing weakly. "Had you fooled, didn't I?"

I'd been set up, as evidenced by the others breaking into laughter.

"Shhhh!" I said, closing the door behind us. "We have to get out of here before there's any of that. Listen up. Let's go over this one more time. Put your masks on now. Sims and Jones will come around to make sure they're nice and tight. When we get downstairs by the guards, I want all of you to imitate what

Captain Goldman just did—only cough toward the guards. That should back them up and keep them from being too curious."

"Make it good, boys," Sims said, shaking his fist in the air. "Cough like dogs!"

"We don't want to sound like a dog kennel," I said, glaring at Sims. "But, let's do put on a little bit of a show. Are you all up for this?"

They all nodded, so I continued. "Sims and I are going to get one of the stretchers over there and take Private Montague down. Jones and Private Scalini will use the other to move Lieutenant Collins. Captain, I know you don't feel well, but that leaves you and Corporal Ernst to get yourselves down behind us. Please, keep hold of each other—and whatever you do, don't fall."

I walked over and stuck my head slowly out the door to check the hallway. Turning around, I said to the men, "Quickly now! Masks on. Tie them tight. And when you get out the door, don't look down toward the other end of the hallway. We don't want anyone to see your masks. Just keep your eyes behind me. Let's do this!"

Sims and I took the lead. Private Montague was slight of build, but I still struggled to keep the stretcher high enough so as not to bump the steps as we made our way down. I glanced back, and it appeared Jones and Private Scalini were having the same issues. Behind them, Captain Goldman was holding Corporal Ernst's hand and carefully guided him step by step.

As soon as we were all down, I called over to the guards, "Put those masks on—now! Hold your breath as long as you can. When you can't any longer, don't breathe out of your mouths. If you feel you must, step back and turn away. Got that?"

Both immediately stood their rifles in the corner and frantically tied on their masks.

"Good boys!" I said as we coughed and hacked our way by. "And go wash your hands and faces soon as we're gone. No sense taking any chances at all. Don't want you to get the TB!"

The tallest of the two shouted through his mask after we were already a fair distance down the sidewalk, "We didn't let anyone in. Sent everyone around to the main entrance. Didn't take any chances."

"Good thinking!" I shouted back. "I'm going to put both of you up for citations for doing that. I'll be back later to get your names. Now, keep those masks on until we're gone!"

When we got to the truck, hoisting the stretchers up while keeping them steady was tough. My arms ached and I felt a twinge in my back, but we finally got Private Montague inside. We then helped Jones and Private Scalini lift in Lieutenant Collins. Captain Goldman, now panting and coughing for real, managed to get in and reached back to help Corporal Ernst climb up. As soon as all were in, Sims said to me, "Get in with 'em. I'll get us to the plane."

The whole evacuation hadn't taken us five minutes, and I didn't think we'd been noticed by anyone except the guards. Still, we weren't home free. We had to get into the air before the hospital room was checked.

Sam was standing at the bottom of the plane's steps as we pulled up, frantically waving us over. "Need to hurry! Let's go!"

Loading everyone was a challenge, one I hadn't anticipated. This was a DC-3, which meant no large cargo door at the rear. It took every ounce of muscle I could muster, and I heard Private Montague groan a few times in the process, but we finally managed to get him inside. Jones and Private Scalini asked Captain Goldman to help them, and soon they had Lieutenant Collins in as well. This plane also had no open space at the rear, as there had been in the *Able Mabel,* so all we could do was move the stretchers back as far as we could and keep them on the floor in the aisle. I carefully stepped around them and helped Corporal Ernst inside.

As soon as all were as secure as we could make them, Sims called forward to the pilot, "Fire it up. Get out of here—fast!"

Sims and Jones came over to me as the engines roared to life. "This is where we get off," Sims said, reaching out to shake my hand. He smiled. "We have to stay here. We're *heroes,* after all."

"You are to me," I said, drawing them to me and hugging them again. "I never could have done this . . ."

"Oh, you'd have figured out a way," Jones cut in. "Turns out you're almost as sneaky as we are."

"Looks like it," I replied, pointing around at the men. "But I don't know what I'm going to do without you now."

"You'll be fine," Sims said, looking toward the cockpit. "Give me a minute."

He walked up to the cockpit, pulled a roll of dollar bills from his pocket, and after handing them to the pilot, he turned and called back to me, "He's going to have mechanical problem later today—and have to land at Bolling Field. I'm sure of it. So, don't worry. You'll make it."

After he walked back to me, he reached into his pocket again and pulled out a pair of dice. "Here. These are for you. Call them a souvenir. If you keep 'em, maybe you won't forget us."

I could feel the tears coming, but the pilot announced, "I'm cleared. Got to go right now."

Sims and Jones quickly climbed out, waved, and headed back to the truck. Sam closed and secured the door, and in a matter of seconds, we were taxiing out for takeoff.

~

Once at our cruising altitude, I walked up to the cockpit to thank the crew. The pilot appeared to be in his mid-thirties. He also looked like he could have used a shave and a clean uniform. The co-pilot didn't look any better—and smelled like he hadn't seen a cake of soap in a while.

"I want to thank you men," I said, reaching out to shake their hands.

"Did you hear somebody talking?" the pilot said to the co-pilot. "Could have sworn I did."

"Nah—was just that right engine again, coughin' and sputterin'."

"I didn't see anybody else get on board, did you?" the pilot continued. He turned and winked at me.

I got the message and headed back to the men. After I sat and tightened my seatbelt, I turned to Sam. "We did it! We really did!"

"Yeah, but what did we do?" he said, rubbing his forehead. "What's going to happen when we get to Bolling Field? That's what I'm wondering. We were *pirates* before. What are they going to say we are now?"

"We'll just have to take it as it comes. Got this far, didn't we? I'm only sorry I got you involved in this mess. Could cost you your stripes, I'll take full responsibility. I'm going to tell them you didn't know anything about this."

"The heck you are. This was *my* idea—and I'll swear to it."

I looked at him, shook my head, and said, "We'll see about that. Right now, first things first. We've got to get there."

Sam nodded and stood to look to the men. We alternated the checks every fifteen minutes just to make sure they were as comfortable as possible.

About an hour and a half into the flight, the co-pilot came back, looked around at the men, but didn't say anything about them. Instead, he turned to me and said, "We're getting ready to land at Norfolk, Virginia. Got to pick up a couple of mechanics who'll be going with us the rest of the way. Don't worry. We just aren't going to say anything about you, so you tell them what you want—if anything."

"Sounds good to me," I replied as he headed back toward the cockpit. "Thank you. Thank you for everything." He didn't turn around. He just waved back and kept going.

When we landed, the mechanics weren't waiting, so the co-pilot went looking for them. "Shouldn't be long," the pilot called back to me. "Just keep yourselves comfortable a few minutes, and we'll be on our way. Sorry about the delay. Can't be helped."

I didn't go into many details about why we had to leave Morrison Field so quickly, but I knew the men were also feeling more than a little anxious. So, to pass the time and offer a little distraction, I reached in my pocket and pulled out the dice Sims had given me. "Boys," I said, holding them in the air, "ever heard of a game called Rinka?" When none of them replied, I said, "It's easy. Here's how the game goes."

For the next few minutes I explained the rules as best I knew them, making up a detail here and there. "Now, I need a volunteer." Private Scalini raised his hand, and I said, "Good.

Now how much do you want to bet I don't throw a multiple of three? Go ahead. Give me an amount. It's only *pretend* money, of course, so don't worry."

"Fifty dollars!" he called out. "And make it real money. I'm good for it." As soon as he did, the others leaned over and became much more interested.

"No, no," I said. "This is just for *educational* purposes right now. We might talk about real bets later, but let's just go with pretend for now. Here we go!"

I rattled the dice several times in my right hand and shot them a foot up the aisle. "Six!" I shouted. "You lose! And fifty real dollars. Thank you, Private Scalini."

"Wait a minute!" he protested. "You said this was just pretend!"

Everyone laughed, loudly, except Corporal Ernst, who did look like he had the faintest hint of a smile. I went around the men, took their imaginary bets, and rolled the dice. They lost a combined four-hundred and ten dollars after just one round.

"Wait a minute! Let me look at those dice!" Private Scalini said when I came back to him. "Something fishy here."

"Why, don't you trust me?" I asked, laughing along with the rest.

"I may trust you, but I'm not so sure about those dice!" was his reply.

"Oh, ye of little faith," I said, shaking my head over and over. The laughter that followed felt good—for us all.

A few minutes later the co-pilot returned with the mechanics following right behind him. The mechanics nodded to Sam and me as soon as they had climbed aboard, but they moved forward to the row right behind the cockpit and belted in. No sooner had they sat down when the engines started again, and we headed back out to the strip. As soon as we had final clearance, we were airborne and quickly leveled off.

I didn't know how much Sims paid the crew, but whatever it was, it surely wasn't enough. Just as Sims told me would happen, they declared engine trouble about thirty miles east of Bolling Field. I was forward and checking to make sure Private Montague's stretcher was still anchored securely, so I heard the radio transmission quite clearly. They didn't declare a state of emergency. All they said—and calmly at that—was one of their engines had suddenly started running rough, and to be on the safe side, they asked for, and received, permission to land at Bolling so they could check it out. Once the exchange had been made, the pilot turned and called me up to the cockpit.

"We won't be down long," he said. "I don't think we'll find much engine trouble. Probably just enough for you to get everybody out the door. So, get yourselves ready. We're starting down now."

"Thank you . . ." was all I could get out before he waved me away.

The landing was smooth, and the stretchers barely moved on the aisle floor as we finally came to a stop. Nobody knew we were coming, so I knew I had some quick work to do.

"Sam, I need to find a couple of men to help with the stretchers. And a truck. You stay here and get everyone lined up. I'll be back fast as I can."

As luck would have it, two privates were sitting in a jeep just a few yards away, I called them over.

"Got some wounded men here," I said, pointing back at the plane. "Need your help to get them out. And, we'll need a truck to get them to Walter Reed."

They just looked at me and didn't move.

"Well, snap to it!" I commanded. "No time to waste. This is an emergency!"

They looked at each other, then back at me. "Yes, Sir! Right away!"

For what seemed like the first time all trip, there were no glitches, no snafus. We arrived at the Admissions entrance at Walter Reed Hospital in twenty minutes. As we pulled up, I jumped out of the truck.

Once inside, I walked right to the Admissions Desk, plopped down my stack of medical charts, and said, "Dropping off. I have some wounded outside."

"You'll have to wait just a minute," the Admitting Nurse said, not looking up as she finished jotting a few notes on a pad of paper.

I started drumming my fingers on the counter. "What's the matter?" she asked again, still not looking at me. "You in a hurry or something?"

"I think you could say that," I said, this time rapping my knuckles next to where she was writing. "Been with these men a long time, and I'll like to get them finally cared for properly."

Putting down her pencil, she looked at me and said, flatly, "OK—how many, and where'd they come from? I'll get the paperwork started."

"Five—from Karachi."

"Where?" she asked. "Kara—what?"

"Karachi," I said, drawing out each syllable. "You know, in *India.*"

"Everyone's funny today," she said, shaking her head. "Come on, where they from?"

"I'm not joking. And there's one more thing I'd like you to do for me. I'm under very strict orders to let Colonel Jackson know the second I get here. He's expecting me."

I paused, smiled, and said, "Well, maybe not exactly like this, but he's still expecting me just the same. Would you please have someone get him on the horn and let him know I'm here?"

"You're serious?" she asked, kicking back her chair as she stood up. "Colonel Jackson is in charge of this whole hospital. He doesn't have anything to do with this end of things."

"He will today," I said, pointing toward the phone. "I guarantee it. Please, make the call."

"All right," she said, again shaking her head. "It's your neck."

Not two minutes later, orderlies came out to help Sam bring in the men. As each was taken past the Admitting Desk, I shook his hand and promised I'd find them all later to make sure they were being treated well. When Corporal Ernst went by, he offered me a small smile. I squeezed his hand, tightly.

As soon as they were all past, I looked up and saw two MPs walking toward me. "I told you it was your neck," the nurse said, laughing softly. "I think you're in for it now."

I just glared at her as the MPs instructed me to follow them. With one on each side of me, we marched down to the very end of the hallway and into Colonel Jackson's office.

As soon as I was shown in, Colonel Jackson didn't introduce himself. He motioned for me to sit down, then barked, pointing to his desk, "That phone line has been burning up all day, Lieutenant. The hospital administrator at Morrison says *somebody* stole some of his patients. Apparently, he saw a letter with my name on it, so he thinks I had something to do with this—and wants somebody arrested for it. Now, I want some answers, and I mean right this minute!"

I knew I shouldn't have interrupted him, but I had to. "But he's not regular Army, Sir. He didn't understand . . ."

"And it's a good thing for you he isn't! Otherwise, those MPs would have taken you right to the stockade."

He paused to let his words sink in. "How in the world did you get here? No, wait—I don't think I want to know. Not now anyway. For now, your patients are what's most important. How they doing? Any problems along the way I should know about?"

When I saw his face soften, I smiled and relaxed a little. I thought about his question, "Any problems along the way?" German fighters, explosions, snipers, saboteurs, plane emergencies . . .

Finally, I looked right at him and said, "No, not too many problems, Sir. Nothing we couldn't take care of. All things considered, a pretty smooth trip, I'd say."

"I bet!" he said, leaning back heavily in his chair. "Someday, you and I are going to have to have a long talk."

He was quiet for a few seconds then smiled. "Just what did you do at Morrison?"

"I made a field decision, Sir," I replied. "I did what I've been trained to do. That's all."

"Well, apparently, it worked, but now I've got a problem to deal with. I've got to throw at least a bone to that administrator."

His smile grew broader. "You're going to have to be *disciplined,* you know. Can't see any way around that. But, I'm still not sure exactly what you did, so I think I better just cover all the bases at once. How about this?

"First of all, we've got to get you out of here. You have to disappear for a while so nobody can find you. What would you say to two weeks of rest and relaxation, effective immediately? Think you could stand that?"

Before I could respond, he continued, "Of course, you'll need to do some reports first—immediately. I have to have those straight away, and I want as much as you can give me while it's all fresh in your mind. I'm going to have to sleep on everything else and decide if any other disciplinary action is warranted. We'll meet again in the morning. Be back right here at exactly zero seven hundred. And none of this disappearing act again. Understood?"

"Yes, Sir," I said. "I'll be here. Don't worry."

"You may go," he said, pointing toward the door.

As I stood to leave, he laughed, shook his head, and said, "Wow, was he mad—the administrator down there. Just how did you . . .? You didn't steal a plane, did you?"

I smiled at him and said, "See you in the morning, Sir."

As I left the office and entered the hallway, I could hear his laughter growing louder and louder.

∾

Chapter 15

Vindications

0651 ZULU, January 24
Walter Reed Hospital, Washington D.C.

The previous evening I had been put up in the nurses' lounge, but I slept very little. I kept thinking about the events at Morrison Field, debating with myself about whether I could have handled the situation differently. I also worried about Sam—and Sims and Jones. I had orders that could cover most of my actions. They didn't. I tossed and turned all night trying to come up with ways to paint them out of the picture, so I could protect them as best I could.

I finally gave up on sleep and decided to find the men and check on them. Even though I had known them only a short time, I felt a bond I knew would not end when we finally had to go our separate ways.

When I got to their room, Private Scalini was already awake and sitting in a chair by the window. I quietly walked over and visited with him. Instead of greeting me, he looked up solemnly and said, "Two are already gone. They came earlier and took Captain Goldman. I heard them say they were going to a tuberculosis sanitarium on the other side of town. A few minutes later, some others came for Private Montague. They told him he was going to a hospital close by where the doctors are having promising results operating on spines. Don't know if they were just trying to cheer him up or were telling the truth, but he seemed happy to be going."

"What are you doing up?" I asked, instinctively reaching over to check his forehead for fever.

"Couldn't sleep. I think this room is, well, too nice—compared to what we've had lately."

I laughed—and immediately covered my mouth so I wouldn't wake the others. "I know what you mean. I actually had a clean blanket last night. But I couldn't sleep, either."

"One more thing," he said, his voice turning serious. "An officer—some Colonel—came in last night and asked us questions about the trip over. We didn't know what you'd want us to tell him, so we all gave him a bunch of rigmarole. Didn't tell him a thing, really, except we got here and all felt good. That was OK, wasn't it?"

"Thanks, Tony," I said. "I still don't know exactly what they want to hear, so I'm keeping mum myself until I do. When the others wake up, please thank them for me. And, more than anything, tell them how proud I am of everyone. And how grateful I am all of you came together and helped me. I'm not going to wake them. I've got to leave. I'm going to be questioned again myself soon. Thanks again for everything. I mean that—with all my heart."

"You don't need to be thanking us," he said, reaching over to shake my hand. "We owe you so much more than we can ever repay. We all know that."

"You take care of yourself, Soldier," I said, starting to turn toward the door. "And get those eyes fixed up good so we can play more Rinka the next time we meet. You still owe me fifty bucks, don't you?"

"I owe you more than that," he said, standing. Snapping to attention, he saluted me. I saluted back and left the room.

I had just two minutes to get to Colonel Jackson's office, so I quickly ran down the steps and down the hall. The receptionist didn't even look up. She pointed toward the door and said, "He's expecting you."

As soon as I was inside, Colonel Jackson ordered me to sit. "You can relax, Lieutenant," he began while shuffling some papers on his desk. "Right after you left yesterday I got on the horn with that administrator down at Morrison, and I don't think he'll be a problem any more. I told him we were taking care of you—that we had something special in mind. That seemed to satisfy him. I think he just wanted to make sure a pound of flesh got thrown around somewhere along the line. So, forget about him."

I fell heavily back in my chair and blew out a breath as he continued. "And I needed some time to see just how much I could share with you about all this. Before I start, though, I want you to know you have some people who really care about you. I had a Sergeant Rigazzi in here about half an hour ago. He said *everything* that happened on the trip was all his fault, that he was as sorry as he could be. He told some pretty wild tales, none of which will show up in your official reports I hope. Understand?"

"Yes, Sir. Perfectly," I replied.

"I also had a written deposition of sorts waiting for me this morning from a Captain Goldman. He said anything that happened not according to plan was all because of his tuberculosis—and everything was his fault. Last evening I went up to visit with your patients, and I couldn't get anything out of them. Why, I couldn't have gotten their mouths open with a tire jack. Loyalty is one thing, but I've never seen anything like that before."

I smiled again. "They're good men, Sir. All of them."

"They might be. But, right now all I know is that there are too many versions of what happened, or didn't happen, on your journey, and that bothers me. I hope your next reports will shed some light here. They had better."

He got up, walked around his desk, and shook my hand, firmly. "What I'm going to say next has to stay in this room for now. I want you to acknowledge you understand this."

"I understand, Sir."

"Lieutenant, you've done a great service for the medical community, the Army Air Forces, and your country—and I, for one, am proud of you."

Those were the last words I expected, so I had no idea what type of response to give. He saw my confusion. "I can tell you now that you were something of a trial balloon—and, we hoped, you'd turn out to be a symbol we really needed. Many of us believe the wounded can be taken great distances to receive specialized care when that's required. But, we needed you to prove it. We needed to make a statement, a *dramatic* one. We also hoped you and your efforts would help initiate deeper discussions of this at every level. We knew if you were successful, we'd have a leg up on what we're aiming to accomplish. By all accounts so far, what you did was a great success."

The gravity of what he said started to hit me. "But, Sir— what if I had failed?" I cut in. "What if . . ."

I started to ask another question, but he motioned for me to remain silent. "You need to hear the rest of this. I'll be perfectly honest with you. This would have been considered a success no matter what happened, as silly as that probably sounds. You see, we learn from our mistakes, so if this had all gone badly, we'd have also known one heck of a lot about what to do in the future to improve. Do you understand that? I'm glad that you were able to do what you did so well. That's going to help us going forward. However, when you do the rest of your reports, don't sugar-coat much. If you feel some concerns should be discussed to make long-range transport more practicable, we want to hear them. No, make that this: We must hear them. Right now, you're the teacher, and we're the pupils. Think of it that way when you write everything down, OK?"

I chose my words carefully, but I just had to say something. "So, Sir, this was all an *experiment?*"

"Of sorts. We hoped it would be more of a *vindication* of our beliefs—a foundation for future progress. Now it appears that's what we've got."

Returning to his chair, he looked directly at me a moment, his face becoming even more serious. "There's one more area for us to discuss this morning. What you did was only the beginning. We've much more to do. Part of it is already taking place, and we'd like you to be involved. We're starting a new program at a base down in Kentucky. We're going to call it either the "Flight Nurse Program" or the "Cadet Nurse Program"—still thinking about that—and it will be for a very select group of nurses we believe have what it takes to build on what you did. We're talking hundreds of nurses in the air, to help give care to the wounded whose chances of survival will increase dramatically if we can get them to the treatment they need in time. Think of the lives we can save. Think of the men who otherwise wouldn't be able to get back home, start their families, and be with their loved ones.

"We want you for this program. We want you to help teach it, to share your experiences—both the good and the not so good—with the other nurses. You can help prepare them for a whole new role in the Army Air Forces, one that can dramatically change the way we care for our wounded. "

He moved out in front of his desk again and stood before me. "Lieutenant Ott, can we count on you? Will you help us move forward?"

I stood. "I'd be deeply honored, Sir. I promise I'll give you my best."

He shook my hand. "Let's do it!"

After saluting him, I left the office. As I started down the hall, I exhaled heavily and thought to myself, *"Flight Nursing school?* Me? Me—who said my feet would never leave the ground again?" I smiled as I thought of the possibilities—and then laughed all the way out of the building. As soon as I entered the morning sunshine, what looked like a C-47 roared overhead, banking to the west.

I saluted, waved—and stood there, watching until it was completely out of sight.

~

Epilogue

The specific distance and time covered by Lieutenant Elsie Ott's journey has been reported with great variation through the years, most likely because of the secrecy involved in both the planning and execution of the mission. However, by most accounts, her journey from Karachi, India, to Walter Reed Hospital covered approximately thirteen thousand air miles and took just over six and a half days. At that time, the same journey with the same patients would have taken close to three and a half months through a combination of ship, truck, and train transport. Through her efforts, Elsie provided exactly the proof the Office of the Air Surgeon hoped would show the benefits and even necessity of evacuating the wounded by air.

She used part of the two-weeks of "rest and relaxation" she was given after the mission to come up with her list of recommendations for preparing nurses for future flights involving the transfer of wounded soldiers. Her recommendations included the following:

✓ A team of medical personnel should meet all planes arriving with patients. This team should relieve the nurse accompanying the patients of all duties while the plane is on the ground.

✓ Food should be furnished by the medical department at each stopping point for use during flight to the next stopping point, so that nurses do not have to procure these items.

✓ A transcript of the medical care given each patient during the stop-overs should be given to the attending nurse for attachment to the clinical records of each patient, to keep all records up-to-date.

✓ Storage containers for all medical files and related documents should be on every plane.

✓ A small medical supply kit weighing 12 to 15 pounds should be sent with each nurse. Each kit should include the following: a supply of 2cc syringes; a container of alcohol; a stimulant such as coramine; pain management medicines such as morphine; spirits of ammonia; aspirin; soda bicarbonate with peppermint (for motion sickness); basic bandages, dressings, and medications.

✓ A supply of oxygen and blankets would be kept readily available at all times.

✓ Thermos bottles or jugs with hot coffee should be procured at each stop.

✓ Nurses should be given sufficient notice before flights in order to pack appropriately and bring along sufficient clothing and personal items.

✓ Aboard planes, mattresses, space permitting, would be more appropriate than litters for patients with limited mobility.

✓ Nurses should not fight, but should be taught to protect themselves if the need arises.

✓ Nurses must be equipped with slacks or a one-piece uniform of such material that will enable them to be presentable even after sleeping in their clothes during an ocean hop. Due to the climbing about to get into and out of the planes and in the care of patients once aboard, a skirt is impracticable.

Virtually all of her recommendations were implemented as soon as it was practical to do so.

After returning from her R&R period, Elsie was assigned to the newly-formed "Air Evacuation Nurse" program at the Air Evacuation School at Bowman Army Air Field in Louisville, Kentucky. The course of study ran for six weeks. She was not just a student in the program; she also helped with the instruction, drawing upon the observations and experience she gained during her historic mission. The curriculum there included instruction in oxygen therapy; administration of anesthesia; how to recognize, prevent, and treat shock; care of psychiatric patients; effects of altitude on physical and mental illnesses; administration of blood and blood derivatives; "ditching" procedures in the event of airplane emergencies; and even "travel hygiene for nurses." Elsie's personal experiences were also used as "What Would You Do in This Situation?" discussion topics during the training sessions. Sections of the flight record she kept during her mission were used as a "supplemental textbook," but, as she had been instructed, many of her experiences were removed from the official record, to the great relief of many.

On March 26, 1943, at Bowman Air Field, in recognition of her accomplishments during her mission, Lieutenant Elsie Ott was awarded the Army Air Medal. She was the first woman ever to receive this honor. The medal was presented by Brigadier General Fred Borum, a staunch supporter of medical air evacuation. Also in attendance was General David Grant, the Army Air Surgeon. It had been his dream that led to the planning for Elsie's historic journey. At the ceremony, the following citation was read as the medal was pinned on her uniform:

Second Lieutenant Elsie S. Ott, Army Nurse Corps, United States Army. For meritorious achievement while participating in an aerial flight from India to the United States January 17 to 23, 1943. During this flight, Lieutenant Ott served as nurse for five patients who were being evacuated from India to Washington, D.C. This was the pioneer movement of hospitalized patients by air over such a great distance. Several of these patients were suffering from serious ailments which required constant attendance and vigilance on the part of Lieutenant Ott. In addition to her nursing duties, she was responsible for arranging for the feeding and housing of the patients en route, the transportation and stowage of their baggage, as well as making all financial arrangements involving their feeding and care while at ground bases not under the control of the Army Air Forces. The successful transportation of these patients was made possible largely by the efficiency and professional skill of Lieutenant Ott and her unflagging devotion to duty. It further demonstrated the practicability of long-range evacuation by air of seriously ill and wounded military personnel from theaters of operations and reflected great credit upon Lieutenant Ott and the Army Nurse Corps.

After the training at Bowman Field, Elsie was officially granted "Air Evacuation Nurse" status and was sent back to Karachi, India, where she was assigned to the 803rd MAES (Medical Air Evacuation Squadron). She continued her pioneering work as a Flight Nurse for the duration of the war, caring for thousands of wounded soldiers transported under her supervision. For her meritorious work in the China-Burma-India theater, she earned the rank of Captain.

Eventually, thirty Medical Air Evacuation Squadrons, all supported by the newly-trained Air Evacuation Nurses, served in WWII. Just over a year after the first nurses graduated from the initial program at Bowman Field, the percentage of wounded evacuated by airplane climbed to nearly twenty percent, with that number increasing steadily throughout the remainder of the war. In total, over 1,172,000 patients were transported by air during the conflict. Of this number, only forty-six patients died in flight. At the same time, seventeen Flight Nurses lost their lives while transporting their patients.

The Air Evacuation Nurse program and those who served within it saved thousands of lives, a legacy that continues to inspire new generations of Flight Nurses in both military and civilian roles.

And what of others who were also involved in the historic flight?

Sergeant Sam Rigazzi, because of his arthritis, was not sent back to India. Instead, he was reassigned to duty at Fort Lee Army Base, Prince George, Virginia, where he remained for the rest of the war. After being discharged, he returned to St. Louis and resumed his work in the family restaurant. He married, had six children, and became a pillar of the Italian community there.

Lieutenant Paul Jordan, Lieutenant Wilbur Dix, and the *Able Mabel* resumed missions, without serious incident, in the China-Burma-India theater the remainder of the war. After his discharge, Lieutenant Jordan began a long and successful career as a commercial airline pilot back in the States. Lieutenant Dix returned to the radio station his father owned in Kentucky, eventually becoming station manager.

Captain Sidney Goldman recovered from his tuberculosis and became a dentist in St. Petersburg, Florida. Private Tony Scalini's glaucoma was successfully treated through a new medical procedure, and he became a taxi driver in New York City, one known for the "adventurous rides" given to his customers. After seven delicate and risky operations, Private Andrew Montague was finally once again able to walk and resume normal activities. He became a minister and settled in a small town in southern Alabama. It took several years after the war, but Lieutenant Jerome Collins recovered from his poliomyelitis enough that he was able to earn his private pilot's license. He served as chief pilot for several corporations until his retirement. Corporal Ed Ernst was initially taken for treatment to a psychiatric hospital outside Washington, D.C. He died just over a year later, the attending coroner listing "natural causes" as the reason for his passing.

For their assistance in helping make the *Able Mabel* airworthy again while at Kano, Privates Jim Sims and Elroy Jones were both recommended for the Silver Star by the Allied command in Accra. However, after a short investigation into the specifics surrounding their activities, the recommendation was withdrawn. After the war, they operated a popular Mediterranean-themed restaurant in Cleveland, Ohio. It was often reported they won the restaurant in a dice game.

After they parted at Morrison Field, Lieutenants Chuck Dunning and Elsie Ott wrote to each other at least once a week, growing closer and closer as they shared their wishes and dreams for the future. However, a shared future was not meant to be. While on a bombing raid of Tokyo, Chuck's B-29 Superfortress took several hits and later crashed into the Pacific Ocean. There were no survivors.

A few years after the war, Elsie took the job of Head Nurse at a hospital in Chicago, Illinois, where she met Larry Mandot, a medical insurance salesman. After a short courtship, they married and moved to Wheaton, Illinois. Several years later, after her husband passed, she returned to Chicago, where she took employment at a private hospital specializing in the care and treatment of WWII veterans.

In the spring of 1968, the Air Force contacted Elsie Ott and asked if she would do the christening for their new C-9A Air Ambulance, the most sophisticated unit ever put together for aeromedical evacuation. She agreed, and on June 17 of that year at Scott Air Force Base outside Belleville, Illinois, she delivered an inspiring address about the history of Flight Nursing before christening the new ship, which was given the designation *Nightingale*.

Elsie eventually moved to Cathedral City, California, where she was reunited with several of her friends who had also served as Flight Nurses during WWII. She and the others volunteered regularly at a Veterans Administration hospital until Elsie's passing, on December 15, 2006. She was 95 years young. As per her request, her ashes were taken to the air and spread over the Pacific Ocean.

Today, the National Museum of the US Air Force, at Wright-Patterson Air Force Base in Dayton, Ohio, has a permanent exhibit honoring Elsie and the other pioneer Flight Nurses who followed. The exhibit reminds all of the truly special and remarkable accomplishments of these trailblazers.

Finally, Lieutenant Elsie Ott passed along a legacy of caring and compassion that provided the foundation for The Flight Nurse's Creed, which is also a fitting memorial to her work and accomplishments:

The Flight Nurse's Creed

I will summon every resource to prevent the triumph of death over life.

I will stand guard over the medicines and equipment entrusted to my care and ensure their proper use.

I will be untiring in the performances of my duties and I will remember that, upon my disposition and spirit, will in large measure depend the morale of my patients.

I will be faithful to my training and to the wisdom handed down to me by those who have gone before me.

I have taken a nurse's oath, reverent in man's mind because of the spirit and work of its creator, Florence Nightingale. She, I remember, was called the "Lady with the Lamp."

It is now my privilege to lift this lamp of hope and faith and courage in my profession to heights not known by her in her time. Together with the help of flight surgeons and surgical technicians, I can set the very skies ablaze with life and promise for the sick, injured, and wounded who are my sacred charges.

This I will do. I will not falter in war or in peace.

Photo Section

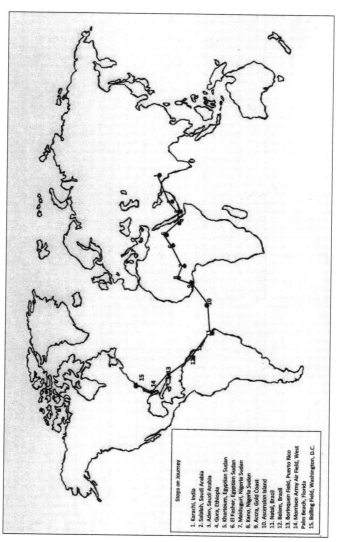

Route Map

Stops on Journey

1. Karachi, India
2. Salalah, Saudi Arabia
3. Aden, Saudi Arabia
4. Gura, Ethiopia
5. Khartoum, Egyptian Sudan
6. El Fasher, Egyptian Sudan
7. Maiduguri, Nigeria Sudan
8. Kano, Nigeria Sudan
9. Accra, Gold Coast
10. Ascension Island
11. Natal, Brazil
12. Belem, Brazil
13. Borinquen Field, Puerto Rico
14. Morrison Army Air Field, West Palm Beach, Florida
15. Bolling Field, Washington, D.C.

General N.W. Grant, Army Air Surgeon. His vision and strong resolution for improved care for wounded and ill soldiers led to Lt. Ott's historic mission, and later the new Air Evacuation Nurse Program. (Photo credit: Courtesy U.S. Army Photo Archives)

The C-47 "Gooney Bird" (above) was the most popular air evacuation aircraft of WWII and was the model used for the first half of Lt. Ott's journey. (Photo credit: Courtesy Douglas Hartley)

The B-24 Liberator (above) was designed to serve as a heavy bomber, but several were redesigned for medical air evacuation and transport, as was the unit used for the second half of Lt. Ott's mission. (Photo credit: Courtesy Copeland Collection)

Lt. Ott, third from the right in middle row, on graduation day at the Air Evacuation School, Bowman Army Air Field, Louisville, Kentucky. On this day she was presented her wings and given the official status and rank of "Air Evacuation Nurse." (Photo credit: Courtesy U.S. Army Photo Archives)

Receiving the Army Air Medal on March 26, 1943, for her determination and courage during her historic mission. The medal is being presented by Brigadier General Fred Borum. Lt. Ott was the first woman to be recognized with this honor. (Photo credit: Courtesy U.S. Army Photo Archives)

Army Air Medal presented to Lt. Elsie S. Ott. (Photo credit: Courtesy Copeland Collection)

Lt. Ott, in her new uniform, shortly after her return to duty in Karachi, India. Based upon Lt. Ott's recommendation after her mission, Flight Nurses were soon allowed to wear either pants or one-piece uniforms in place of skirts. Lt. Ott is also shown here preparing a C-47 for aeromedical transport duty. (Photo credit: Courtesy Copeland Collection)

Air Evacuation Nurse Flight Wings (Left) presented to the nurses upon graduation at the new Air Evacuation School Program. (Photo credit: Courtesy Copeland Collection)

803rd MAES (Medical Air Evacuation Squadron) patch (right) presented to Lt. Ott upon her return to duty in Karachi. Note the flying bees carrying the stretcher. (Photo credit: Courtesy Copeand Collection)

Lt. Ott (far right) and other nurses relaxing at the 159th Station Hospital, Karachi, India, after return to duty there as a member of the 803 MAES. (Photo credit: Courtesy U.S. Army Photo Archives)

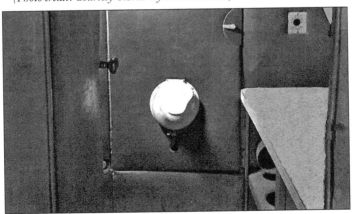

One of the problems faced by women flying aboard the C-47 Transport was the "relief hole." After the flight, one of Lt. Ott's recommendations was proper toilet facilities be designed for both genders. (Photo credit: Courtesy Copeland Collection)

Lt. Ott and her accomplishments served as the inspiration for the recruitment efforts that followed her mission, including posters such as this one. (Photo credit: Courtesy U.S. Army Photo Archives)

Acknowledgments

This book could not have been written without the generous assistance of many wonderful people, all of whom gave freely of their time and knowledge.

For assistance with military history and locating military records and documents, I'd like to thank the following individuals and groups:

First and foremost, I'd like to thank Michael Burke, Lt. Col., U.S. Army, retired, for his insights into military history, his assistance locating difficult to find Army Air Service documents, and putting up with all my questions about military terminology and traditions.

Judith Barger, author of *Beyond the Call of Duty: Army Flight Nursing in World War II,* for providing essential military records and historical background (and inspiration from her articles about WWII Flight Nurses).

Nancy Polette, author of *Angels on Board: Heroic Flight Nurses of World War II,* for research assistance and military history.

Danielle Almeter, Public Affairs Division, National Museum of the Air Force, Wright-Patterson AFB OH, for help sourcing military records of WWII Flight Nurses.

Mary Hope, Senior Archivist, Army Medical Department Center of History and Heritage

Fort Sam Houston, TX, for assistance with military documents.

Judith Taylor, DAFC, Senior Historian, Air Force Medical Service, Lackland AFB, TX, for information about archival flight footage and C-9 history.

U.S. Army Medical Department Center and School Health Readiness Center of Excellence, Fort Sam Houston, Texas (AMEDDC&S ARCoE), for access to former classified military documents and medical records.

U.S. Army Heritage and Education Center, Carlisle Barracks, Pennsylvania, for information related to the Aeromedical Evacuation Nurse Program.

Melinda Bruckman, President of the Legends of the Flight Nurses of World War II Association (http://www.legendsof-flightnurses.org), for documents related to history of aeromedical evacuation.

Tammy Horton and the many historians and researchers at the Air Force Historical Research Agency, Maxwell Air Force Base, for historical documents and military records.

Coby Ellison, Museum Curator, Museum of Transportation, St. Louis, Missouri, for providing specifications of WWII military aircraft (and allowing me to explore the inside of a WWII C-47 transport plane).

Tony Petruso, Overlord Military Collectables, St. Louis, Missouri, for providing military artifacts and history.

Tom Knox, Alamo Military Collectables, St. Louis, Missouri, for information about Flight Nurse uniforms of WWII.

Jason Stratman, Librarian and Research Specialist, Missouri Historical Society Library and Research Center, for helping secure news accounts and historical information related to the WWII Flight Nurse Program.

In addition, I'd like to thank the following for their assistance in locating other historical documents, photographs, and help with manuscript preparation:

The many Research Librarians at the Library of Congress who helped source historical documents and records of the period covered in the story.

Maryana Britt, Artist, for her inspirational drawings and illustrations.

Douglas Hartley for his beautiful photographs and image collection.

Brock Swarbrick, for design consultation and manuscript preparation.

Stan Lyle, Librarian Emeritus, University of Northern Iowa, for his help tracking down very difficult to find maps of the period.

Corrine Holke-Farnam, University of Northern Iowa, for tech support and assistance.

Julie Huffman Klinkowitz, forensic genealogist, for uncovering vital biographical information.

I would also like to offer special thanks to my wife, Linda, for her editorial assistance all through the project—and for tolerating the mounds of books and research documents stacked all over the house—and for her support and encouragement during the large number of trips made to gather research for the project.

And, finally, I'd like to thank Rosemary Yokoi, the best editor and friend a writer ever had!

Thank you, and bless you all!

About the Author

JEFFREY S. COPELAND is a professor in the Department of Languages and Literatures at the University of Northern Iowa, where he teaches courses in literature and English Education. He has authored numerous books, including *Inman's War: A Soldier's Story of Life in a Colored Battalion in WWII*; *Olivia's Story: The Conspiracy of Heroes Behind Shelley v. Kraemer*; *Shell Games: The Life and Times of Pearl McGill, Industrial Spy and Pioneer Labor Activist*; *Ain't No Harm to Kill the Devil: The Life and Legend of John Fairfield, Abolitionist for Hire*; *I'm Published! Now What? An Author's Guide to Creating Successful Book Events, Readings, and Promotions:* and *Plague in Paradise: The Black Death in Los Angeles, 1924*. He lives in Cedar Falls, Iowa.